LITTLE PIE COMPANY
OF THE BIG APPLE

Pies and Other Dessert Favorites

LITTLE PIE COMPANY
OF THE BIG APPLE

Pies and Other Dessert Favorites

Arnold Wilkerson, Patricia Henly, and Michael Deraney
with Evie Righter

Illustrations by Michael Deraney

HarperPerennial
A Division of HarperCollinsPublishers

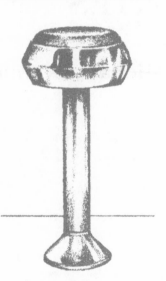

THE LITTLE PIE COMPANY OF THE BIG APPLE PIES AND OTHER DESSERT FAVORITES. Copyright ©
1993 by Arnold Wilkerson, Patricia Henly, and Michael Deraney. All rights reserved. Printed
in the United States of America. No part of this book may be used or reproduced in any manner
whatsoever without written permission except in the case of brief quotations embodied in
critical articles and reviews. For information address HarperCollins Publishers, Inc., 10 East
53rd Street, New York, NY 10022.

HarperCollins books may be purchased for educational, business, or sales promotional use. For
information please write: Special Markets Department, HarperCollins Publishers, Inc., 10 East
53rd Street, New York, NY 10022.

Illustrations copyright © 1993 by Michael Deraney

FIRST EDITION

DESIGNED BY HELENE BERINSKY

Library of Congress Cataloging-in-Publication Data

Wilkerson, Arnold, 1943–
    The Little Pie Company of the Big Apple pies and other dessert
favorites / Arnold Wilkerson, Patricia Henly, and Michael Deraney
with Evie Righter; illustrations by Michael Deraney. —1st. ed.
        p.   cm.
    Includes index.
    ISBN 0-06-095031-5
    1. Pies. 2. Cake. 3. Desserts. 4. Little Pie Company of the Big
Apple. I. Henly, Patricia, 1952– . II. Deraney, Michael J.
III. Title.
TX773.W65   1993   93-7378
641.8'652—dc20

93 94 95 96 97 CC/RRD 10 9 8 7 6 5 4 3 2 1

We dedicate this book to our families

A.W., P.H., M.D.

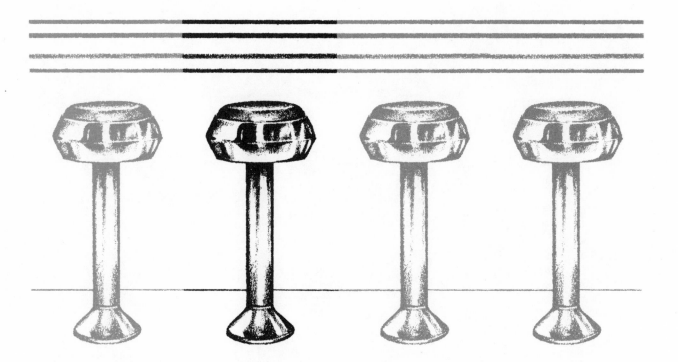

$\mathscr{C}$ONTENTS

$\mathcal{A}$CKNOWLEDGMENTS

Arnold Wilkerson:

I wish to thank my mother, Ms. Bobbie J. Houston, my grandmother, Ms. Jessie Brown, and each of my brothers and sisters. They have always been there with their support and encouragement.

I'd also like to thank my wonderful friends William Kaufmann, Howard Henderson, Michael Deraney, Robert Nahas, and Mark Gittelman, for help making a dream become a reality. And special thanks to my friend and banker Jane Stanicki, and to the Urban Business Assistance Corporation. And warm regards for my teachers Miss Emily Murry and Mr. Michael Powers.

Patricia Henly:

Many thanks to the Little Pie Company's baking, retail, and maintenance staff, who not only shouldered a portion of my responsibilities while I worked on this book but also sampled the desserts and contributed their valued opinions.

Thanks to R. Dianne Reade, our cookbook assistant, who helped with the recipe trials—often working from rough handwritten drafts—for all her wise and intelligent suggestions.

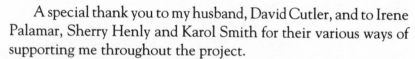

A special thank you to my husband, David Cutler, and to Irene Palamar, Sherry Henly and Karol Smith for their various ways of supporting me throughout the project.

Many thank you's to Evie Righter, with whom it is a true pleasure to work. I learned much from her and am very grateful. Thank you also to her husband, David Talbot, for all the long drives to deliver manuscript.

Michael Deraney:

Many people are responsible for the development of the Little Pie Company as a business. On behalf of past and present employees, I would like to express our gratitude to the Manhattan Plaza professionals Irving Fisher, Rodney Kirk, and Richard Hunnings for their continued support and guidance.

Thank you to Mark Gittelman, Karol A. Smith, and Chris Caswell, developmental team members who have helped to make the Company work behind the scenes.

A special thanks to the beautiful collage of employees who have come and gone over the years. Reminders of their importance in this collaboration appear often and are never forgotten.

FOREWORD

I can't claim to be any sort of an expert on cookbooks, but I do know something about pies. For a couple of years, I even baked them in the Broadway musical *Sweeney Todd*. As Stephen Sondheim put it in one of his marvelous songs, Mrs. Lovett made probably "the worst pies in London." But some years later, I discovered a shop that baked absolutely the best pies in New York: the Little Pie Company.

I was walking down 43rd Street in Manhattan one day when suddenly the scent of baking apples and burnt sugar curled around my nose and led me to a small bakery nestled along a promenade between twin high rises known as Manhattan Plaza. My husband and I had returned to America from Ireland and we had just moved into an apartment there. They call Manhattan Plaza "the miracle on 42nd Street" and it is one of the great habitats of all time because of the splendid sense of community and caring among the residents, many of whom are in the performing arts. Even so, I was still surprised to discover in this urban neighborhood aromas that took me right back to my childhood and to the cozy warmth of my mother's kitchen.

I became hooked on the Little Pie Company before I ever set foot in the door. From the sidewalk, the whole bustling operation was exposed to passersby through the shop's large windows. I could see cooks in white caps and aprons peeling, slicing, and arranging the fruit, pouring the filling into crusts, and placing the pies into gleaming aluminum ovens. Nearby, rows and rows of pies with swollen golden-brown crusts were cooling on racks, one or two periodically snatched up to be taken home or consumed on the spot at a counter in the front of the shop. The windows themselves were decorated to celebrate the season. I think there was a Maypole at the time of my first visit, its colored streamers fanning out and bidding welcome. The sight was theatrical without being hokey, cheery yet down-to-earth, and very, very inviting.

I went in and had something to satisfy my senses, which by that time were reeling—waistline be damned! I chose a piece of carrot cake and bought a berry pie to take home to Peter. On that first visit, I met the owners of the Little Pie Company, Arnold Wilkerson and Michael Deraney, and wasn't surprised to learn that on top of being perfectly charming gentlemen they were also creative. Arnold had been an actor and Michael was, and still is, an illustrator of children's books. If the Little Pie Company is more than just a bakery, it's because both of these young men are highly sympathetic to the rhythms of the universe. As spring turns to summer and summer to fall, I always look forward to seeing not only how the season will be heralded in their windows, but also how the menu will reflect those changes. In summer there are fresh berry pies, in winter warm pecan, in fall pumpkin, of course, and the arrival of spring always means strawberry-rhubarb. During Jewish holidays, there are Passover cakes and on the Fourth of July what could be more American than, well, apple pie.

Whenever I have guests, I rely on the Little Pie Company to provide my dessert, preferring those individual pies in order to give people a choice. When anybody asks if I've baked them, I am sorely tempted to take credit. If the truth be known, I've always secretly aspired to be a good pastry chef. By the time I was seven, just old enough to turn on the electric oven in our London flat, I was taught to make a three-egg cake by my mother, who in turn had been taught by her mother. I suppose I learned from them to be a purist. Anything premixed was absolutely anathema in our house. That is why I hold a place like the Little Pie Company in such awe—I know the time and care and patience it takes to come up with such tempting goods.

Day after day, those cooks turn in a performance of sorts, and it's an extremely high-quality one. They don't go for the quick hit and they don't stop to applaud themselves. After all, whether you're talking about acting or baking, it all comes down to the truth. *Essence* is a word that applies to both the cook and the actor. And if you ask me, knowing the basics of a good muffin or a good pie ranks right up there with the greatest of star turns. So to all my friends at the Little Pie Company at Manhattan Plaza, "Bravo!" And now with this cookbook to help all of us struggling pastry chefs, I might add, "Break a leg!" (Or maybe that should be "Break an egg!")

ANGELA LANSBURY

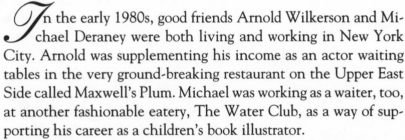

$\mathscr{P}$REFACE

$\mathscr{I}$n the early 1980s, good friends Arnold Wilkerson and Michael Deraney were both living and working in New York City. Arnold was supplementing his income as an actor waiting tables in the very ground-breaking restaurant on the Upper East Side called Maxwell's Plum. Michael was working as a waiter, too, at another fashionable eatery, The Water Club, as a way of supporting his career as a children's book illustrator.

It was a wonderful time to be in New York City, otherwise known as the Big Apple. You could feel the entrepreneurial spirit crackling in the air. Businesses were booming. Restaurants were filled. Food stores could not stock enough exotica—fruits from New Zealand, sweet butter from France, chocolate from Belgium. To have friends in for dinner was to plan an event.

For Arnold and Michael, witnesses to the phenomenal fervor surrounding food, something, strangely, was missing. Arnold had grown up in California, not far from Bakersfield, in rural America, where his grandmother, especially, and his mother, too, would take from the land what they would prepare for dinner. If you wanted apricot cobbler for dessert, you began by picking the apricots yourself or, if Arnold were back from school, asking him to run out and do it. Arnold's grandmother would make her own sausage, put up her own jams and jellies, and bake pies that no one who ever tasted them could forget. Similarly, Michael had grown up in the rural Midwest, in North Dakota. One of seven children, he was reared with the values Arnold was: You do your part; hard work counts; honesty is everything—the American work ethic, untarnished by the glitter of greed or the fast living of a metropolis. Spring came and you picked rhubarb; it was as basic as that.

What was missing for each of them, they would figure out after discussions and analysis and careful thought and lots of eating out, was the food of their childhoods—the simple, pleasing dishes that meant home and a straightforward, reassuring kind of happiness. With that realization, more a discovery than anything else, their entrepreneurial spirits went into high gear. They thought first of going into business to open a restaurant that would only serve breakfasts, great American breakfasts—fresh eggs, bacon, with homemade toasts and jellies, or buttermilk pancakes—the breakfasts they knew from their childhoods. The idea of a diner also appealed: Good, simple, affordable American food would be served in a friendly, no-frills atmosphere to a clientele they hoped would grow to see the diner as the "neighborhood place"—the way it used to be.

While these ideas and others perked, Arnold would cook dinner for his friends, a way of seeing what dishes worked best and just as importantly which drew the most raves—menu research, in effect. Unfailingly, his desserts, and a pie, in particular, won hands down. The thought occurred—maybe they could market that pie. Maybe that pie was what they had to offer.

Months would go by. But no pie. Unflaggingly, Michael would ask Arnold when was he going to make the pie so that he could take it round to restaurants to learn its appeal. One day finally Arnold did. He went to his apartment and baked the pie. With it barely cooled, he then took it down to the restaurant Curtain Up, which was on the street level of his apartment building. He sold that pie immediately, and the next day there was an order for more. Word got out about that wonderful pie, and orders poured in, assisted by a write-up in *New York* magazine that provided more orders than were humanly doable.

As destiny would have it, at just about this time, a friend of Michael's said her sister was thinking about coming to New York City and if she did would be looking for a job. Michael asked nonchalantly what she did. It turned out she was an expert baker. Patricia Henly came to New York and took the job with Arnold Wilkerson and has been baking, in charge of all production, with him ever since.

It quickly became very clear to Arnold, Patricia, and Michael that a commercial space for baking was needed. To begin with, Arnold had had to have the oven in his apartment replaced several times in a matter of two years; the walls, once white, were now an identifiable shade of cinnamon; and the aroma of apples baking, delicious as it was, could be traced directly to his door. Even when Arnold entered the building with a crate of apples on his shoulder, the building management still did not say anything. There was a limit, Arnold was first to admit, as to how long their noblesse oblige attitude could be expected to last.

Never underestimate the viability of word of mouth in a place like New York City, for it was by this that Arnold learned of a storefront that was available on the very block on which he lived. The 500-square-foot former printing shop needed renovation and fixing up, and fortunately Michael was good at all of that, a very handy feature given that the budget they had for getting into business was small and what you could contribute with your own hands was money in the till toward a piece of equipment or the next month's rent. It was at about this time that Arnold, on a ride to New Jersey, something he did every now and then to relax, came up with the name of their enterprise: the Little Pie Company of the Big Apple—little because, literally, that is what it was, and of the Big Apple, for the obvious reason. It was also decided that all their products would be American—as American as apple pie.

That was back in 1984. Since then, the Little Pie Company has moved again—same block, more space—and expanded that space as well. It has also broadened its list of products and departed from an original premise of having apples in every offering. Welcome to cheesecake, lemon pound cake, walnut fudge pie, and so much more! Little Pie Company pies have been enjoyed as far away as Japan and have been delivered on a regular basis to the casts of Broadway shows. The company has even served as the site of a child's birthday party.

What hasn't changed is the philosophy of the company that was so carefully arrived at during those long discussions Arnold and Michael shared before going into business: That simplicity, warmth, and humor, among the principals and always with the customers, would prevail on a daily basis; that quality would never be compromised; that the staff—and it would be a multiracial one—would be treated as important participants, with their opinions counting. The goal? To make American desserts day in and day out the way grandmothers and mothers used to have the time to make them—by hand, with the freshest ingredients and the purest flavors—as if you were serving a friend.

Cleverly, and this has been the way it has been since the door opened, Arnold, Michael, and Patricia each does what he or she does best. Arnold contributes creatively, participating on product development, and sells, Michael handles the business end of things and the people side, and Patricia is responsible for developing the recipes, for managing, baking, and controlling the quality of each product as well as training the baking staff. In short, it is the sum of the parts that equals the whole.

Which brings us to this book. For a while, the Little Pie Company contemplated franchising, and when that was voted down as a business decision for 1992, it was decided to "branch out" instead with a book, a collection of recipes that have been made and are still being made daily at the company on West 43rd Street in Manhattan. Not surprisingly, there are a lot of pie recipes, particularly apple pies, and ones made with fresh fruit. There are also some lighter-than-air cream, custard, and curd pies. There are cakes as well, and finally a selection of what Arnold, Michael, and Patricia call "American favorites"—comforting, sweet combinations, many of them fruit that will remind you of fall days or that spring one, when the rhubarb was ready for picking. Many of these desserts you will remember from your youth, when the pleasure of a splendidly home-baked dessert equaled happiness in an old-fashioned, but hardly antiquated, way. When you undertake these simple recipes, envision the expressions of the two bakers on the logo of the Little Pie Company. The roundish fellows, in chef's attire, but with whimsical, pointed, wizardlike slippers, are each holding an apple in his hand and contemplating it with a bemused, gentle look on his face. Clearly, for these bakers, the anticipated pleasures are limitless. So, we hope, will you find the pleasures of this book.

LITTLE PIE COMPANY
OF THE BIG APPLE

Pies and Other Dessert Favorites

$\mathscr{I}$NTRODUCTION

About the Ingredients

All-Purpose Flour

Both unbleached and bleached all-purpose, nationally available brands of flour were used in developing and testing the recipes that follow. Read each recipe carefully and use only the type of flour listed for the best results.

At the Little Pie Company we weigh our ingredients on either a baker's balance scale or a spring-type scale. We depend on them for the accuracy required in baking. Many home kitchens, however, do not have a reliable kitchen scale. Hence, for the recipes here we use the "stir and spoon" method to measure flour: With a large spoon, stir the flour in the canister or bag a few times to lighten it. Heap the spoon with flour and empty it into a dry measuring cup. Then, when the cup is heaping full, level off the top of

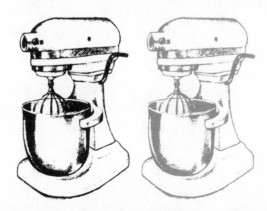

the measuring cup with a single sweep of a straight-edged spatula. When "sifted" flour is called for, the flour should first be sifted onto a piece of wax paper or into a bowl and then lightly spooned into a dry measuring cup. Level off the measure with a spatula as described above.

Baking Powder

This ingredient is a leavening agent and is frequently called for in cakes, quick breads, muffins, and cookies. Buy baking powder in a quantity you think you will use in a year's time. Also, check the can for its expiration date. Time, humidity, and moisture all cause baking powder to lose its strength. To test its potency, mix 1 teaspoon baking powder into 1/4 cup hot water. The mixture should foam. If it does not, it is time to replace your powder.

When measuring, use a clean, dry measuring spoon and always be sure to close the lid tightly after each use.

Butter

The recipes that follow specify unsalted butter. Do not substitute salted butter. When the recipe calls for "softened" butter, use butter that has stood at room temperature (or has been microwaved) until it offers no resistance when you touch it with your finger. It should be neither oily nor partially melted. Chilled butter means just that—straight out of the refrigerator. Frozen and partially thawed butter is used in pie dough recipes that are mixed in the food processor. In these instances, butter that is taken directly from the freezer may be too hard to be safely cut into 1- or 1/2-inch pieces. Let it thaw for a few minutes first. The point is that it should be colder and firmer than chilled for processor-made pie dough.

Cake Flour

Be careful here. You want cake flour—not self-rising cake flour. It is available in 2-pound boxes and should always be sifted before measuring. If a recipe calls for cake flour and all you have on hand is all-purpose flour, use it, but know that the crumb of the cake will be slightly heavier.

Chocolate

Use the best quality available to you in a brand that you like. Store it tightly wrapped in a cool, dry place or in an airtight container, not in the refrigerator.

To melt, heat it, uncovered, over hot—never boiling—water or in a microwave oven on high power, stirring frequently.

Cocoa Powder

Use only unsweetened, preferably Dutch process cocoa powder. Alkali has been added to it, making it darker and milder.

Eggs

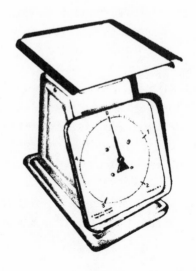

Only Grade A large eggs were used in developing and testing the recipes in this book. Do not substitute extra-large, medium, or small eggs. Eggs in general require careful handling. Only purchase refrigerated eggs and store them at home in the refrigerator. Never use eggs that are cracked or broken.

When a recipe calls for eggs at room temperature, take them out of the refrigerator no more than 1 hour before using. Know that it is easier to separate eggs when they are cold, then let them come to room temperature. To take the chill off quickly, place the bowl of eggs for a few minutes over a pan of warm—not hot—water, and stir them occasionally.

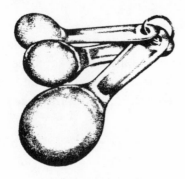

Lard

We use lard in two of our pie dough recipes for its excellent results: a flavor that is complementary to apple and other fruit pies and because it renders the dough easy to handle. Lard is sold in pound packages in the refrigerator sections of large supermarkets. It should smell fresh and pleasing. If it doesn't, substitute solid vegetable shortening.

Pure Vanilla Extract

There is pure vanilla extract and a flavored imitation, which is considerably cheaper than the pure variety. In the recipes that follow, use only the pure extract.

Spices

You will see that ground cinnamon, grated nutmeg, allspice, and various other spices are called for frequently in the pages ahead. To keep them fresh and full-flavored, store ground spices in a cool, dark place, never in a cabinet over the stove or on a shelf exposed to bright sunlight.

Sugar

LIGHT AND DARK BROWN SUGAR: Dark brown sugar has a richer, more caramelly flavor than light brown sugar. For best results, do not substitute one for the other. Always measure either type of brown sugar by firmly packing it into a dry measuring cup and leveling it off with a straight-sided spatula.

CONFECTIONERS' SUGAR: This is also called "powdered" or "confectionery" sugar and has a small amount of cornstarch

added to prevent it from lumping. It is used most often in making icings and for garnishing.

SUPERFINE SUGAR: This very finely processed sugar is only available in a 1-pound box with a metal spout on the side. Because it dissolves almost instantly, it is excellent for use in cake batters and meringues.

Tapioca

In the recipes we call for instant tapioca, which is not to be confused with pearl tapioca. A granular thickener, it is derived from processing the root of the cassava plant. We use tapioca in many of our fresh fruit pies because we especially like the old-fashioned look of the beautifully clear and slightly textured juices it produces. Tapioca is available in 8-ounce boxes in the pudding section of the supermarket or grocery store.

Vegetable Oil

Corn, canola, and safflower oils were used in developing and testing the recipes. It is best to buy vegetable oil in a reasonably sized bottle that you can expect to finish in a timely fashion. If opened, then left to stand indefinitely on the shelf, the oil will turn rancid.

Vegetable Shortening

A nationally available brand of hydrogenated solid vegetable shortening was used in developing and testing the recipes. When using vegetable shortening to make pie dough, remember to measure it and chill it first. Vegetable shortening should be stored on the shelf.

To Lighten the Baker's Load

What follows is a selective listing of equipment that will make your baking easier and more pleasurable. Also look at the suggestions of recommended equipment that precede each chapter for more ideas.

Bench Scraper

This is a rectangular scraper with a straight blunt edge of stainless steel that is used to both efficiently and quickly remove bits of pastry sticking to the rolling surface. At kitchen supply stores you will also find plastic bench scrapers, which tend to be less expensive than the metal variety. They work well, too.

Electric Mixer

A hand-held electric mixer can be used for any of the recipes in this book. If you have a countertop mixer, know that it is likely to be a more powerful and thorough mixer than a hand-held model. In most recipes here we direct the cook to use visual observation to determine the length of the mixing time; it is safer and simpler than relying on the clock when the variables of mixer speed and power are involved.

Food Processor

This high-speed versatile kitchen machine of the twentieth century is invaluable when making certain pastry recipes, for chopping, and in mixing some of the fillings. The batter for New York Cheesecake (page 168) can be made with the food processor in a matter of minutes.

Mercury Oven Thermometer

The temperature of your oven must be accurate, for a too-hot oven or a too-cool one or one with hot spots can mean the ruin of a recipe. A mercury oven thermometer, available in kitchenware stores, is the best piece of equipment for checking oven temperature. Always use it and rely upon it. Also, know your oven's idiosyncracies: Does it seem to be hotter in the back than in the front? On the left side or on the right? If it seems off, get the oven calibrated. Finally, consider the recommended baking time for a recipe as a guideline, and not the last word. Never leave something baking in the oven unattended. Check on it, either through the oven window or open the door for a quick look about 10 minutes before the end of the baking time.

Pastry Brush

Needed for applying glazes to lattice strips and pie tops, this brush is preferably made of natural bristles and comes in a variety of widths. We recommend one 1 1/2 inches wide. Wash it in warm sudsy water, then rinse it well under running water. Shake off the excess water and reshape the bristles with your hand. Allow the brush to air-dry.

Pastry Wheel

If you take special pride in your latticetop pies you may want this simple, old-time tool—a handle with a fluted-edged wheel at the end of it—that gives the strips a particularly pretty look. A pizza cutter or sharp knife will work just as well, but not as decoratively.

Pie Plates

All the recipes in this book were tested in either a standard 9-inch ovenproof glass pie plate or a deep 9-inch ovenproof glass pie plate, the difference being that the standard size holds 4 cups liquid volume, whereas the deeper plate will hold about 5 cups liquid. We prefer clear ovenproof glass pie plates in that they are widely available, reliable, and sturdy, and are pretty for serving as well. In the event you use a metal pie plate, figure that the baking time may be lengthened 5 minutes or so, depending upon the type of metal pan being used.

Rolling Pin

There are any number of different kinds of rolling pins, but we prefer the heavy ball-bearing type with a perfectly smooth surface. As to weight and size, select one that is comfortable for you. After using, wipe the pin clean with a paper towel. Never wash it.

Sifter

This piece of equipment affects measurement, namely the amount of dry ingredients and especially flour, and is therefore much more important than its simple almost rustic design might suggest. If you don't have a sifter, a simple fine-meshed sieve can be used instead. Push the dry ingredients through it with a spoon. Wash a sifter only when necessary; most often it will suffice to simply bang any remaining flour out with your hand.

Wire Rack

Available in kitchenware stores in a variety of shapes (round or square) and sizes, this cooling device is essential in preventing soggy-bottomed pies and in cooling cake layers and loaf cakes.

Wire Whisk

Like rolling pins, wire whisks come in many sizes. They are excellent for stirring together dry ingredients and for beating egg whites and combining liquid ingredients.

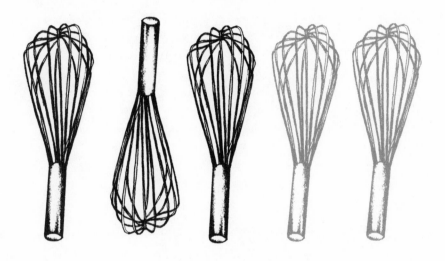

Pies

$\mathscr{A}$PPLE $\mathscr{P}$IES

My favorite cookbook? Oh, that's easy, it's a sentimental favorite, the 1950 Betty Crocker's Picture Cook Book. *It was the one my mother learned to cook from. Then she taught me from it. I thought that all those pictures and illustrations were great! And all the recipes worked.*

—*P.H.*

We started with one apple pie, in 1982, made by one baker (Arnold). At that time we decided to create an all-apple bakery. Over the years we gradually upped the offerings on our list until now we have a dozen or so apple pies that we rotate on and off the menu, depending upon the season. It was a challenge to develop a whole selection of apple pies so that each would be different from the others; so that no filling or texture would duplicate; so that even the look of each pie would be unique.

We began by experimenting with the obvious—apples: which ones had the best flavor, which the best baking qualities, which, very importantly, were most readily available. Next, we started testing doughs. We could choose among single-crust, double-crust, crumb-top combinations. We could use dried apples, too. We had to decide when to be nostalgic and when to be sophisticated. We had to keep the quality top-notch at all times.

One thing we were all sure of, though. Each of us had a very specific idea about what the perfect apple pie was made of. It stood tall and proud. It had a magnificent crust, and it was brimming with fragrant but simply spiced apples. That recipe, Old-Fashioned Apple Pie, begins this chapter. We urge you, though, to try all the other apple combinations that follow it.

BASIC EQUIPMENT

9-inch glass pie plate
Apple corer
Curved blade paring knife
Several good sharp knives
Sturdy cutting board

NICE TO HAVE ON HAND BUT NOT ESSENTIAL

Lemon reamer

I was watching a talk show on the television one day and I will never forget that there was a fellow on talking about how it used to be in America. He said, "At one time in this country, if you wanted to drive a cab, you went out, painted TAXI on your car door, and started to drive." It dawned on me that I could do that with a pie.

—*A.W.*

Old-Fashioned Apple Pie

One 9-inch double-crust pie

Old-Fashioned Dough (page
    111)

6 or 7 large Golden Delicious
    apples, or 3 pounds
1/4 cup light brown sugar,
    firmly packed
1/4 cup granulated sugar, plus
    additional for sprinkling on
    the top crust
2 tablespoons cornstarch
3/4 teaspoon ground cinnamon
1/8 teaspoon grated nutmeg
1 1/2 tablespoons freshly
    squeezed lemon juice
2 tablespoons unsalted butter,
    softened
Egg glaze made by beating
    together well 1 large egg and
    3 tablespoons cold water
Vanilla ice cream, as
    accompaniment

*O*ld-fashioned apple pie was on our menu opening day. This pie, like most of our pies, is made in three sizes, but the granddaddy of them all is the 10-inch old-fashioned apple pie. It has a beautifully browned, sugar-sprinkled, high-standing dome with three pastry leaves on the top. As we make it—high as it is—the pie would be an unwieldy undertaking for home bakers. (Mounding the apples alone takes some practice.) So, the recipe that follows is in the Little Pie Company style, but with less filling.

For those who want *exactly* the same pie, here is how to do it: Increase all the ingredients in the filling by one-third. For example, use 4 pounds Golden Delicious apples, and when it comes time to mound them in the shell don't be discouraged if they tumble out. Just place them gently back in. Also, you will need a 9-inch deep-dish pie plate. Finally, bake the pie in the lower third of the oven at 375°F. for an additional 15 to 20 minutes.

1. Preheat the oven to 425° F.

2. Quarter, core, and peel the apples. Cut each quarter into 3 wedges. Measure the apples into a large bowl. They will make roughly 8 cups.

In the early days of the company, I used to get some of my best ideas while riding on a bus to New Jersey. I'd get on the bus and take the ride just for the opportunity to relax and think. The bus was restful, quiet, and cool. On one of those rides, it occurred to me that what we had in the making, back at the apartment, was a little pie company. I brought this idea back to Mike and he suggested why don't we call it the Little Pie Company of the Big Apple. It was then we agreed to establish the first all-apple bakery in the city.

—A.W.

3. In a small bowl, stir together with a wire whisk the sugars, cornstarch, cinnamon, and nutmeg.

4. Add the lemon juice and the sugar mixture to the apple slices and mix until they are evenly coated.

5. Line the pie plate with the bottom crust and mound the apple filling into it. Using both hands, press and shape the apples to form a tightly packed, high mound. Trim the bottom crust to a 1/2-inch overhang. Dot the filling with butter. Arrange the top crust over the apples, patting the crust gently with your hands, so it conforms to the shape of the filling. Leave a 1-inch edge. Fold the top crust under the edge of the bottom crust and flute the edges decoratively, pressing together with your thumb and forefinger.

6. Reroll the pastry scraps to make 3 large diamond-shaped leaves, each about 2 1/2 inches long. Cut them out freehand or use a diamond-shaped cookie cutter. Use the back of a paring knife to make indentations simulating leaf veins. Brush the backs of the

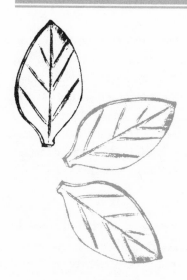

leaves lightly with egg glaze, then apply the leaves to the very top of the pastry, bending or twisting them slightly to give them a natural look. With a sharp paring knife, make 5 or 6 steam vents, each 3/4-inch long, around the center of the top crust.

7. Bake the pie for 20 minutes. Reduce the oven temperature to 375°F. and continue to bake the pie for 40 minutes. Ten minutes before the end of the baking time, brush the top with egg glaze and sprinkle with sugar. The pie is done when the pastry is golden brown and the juices are bubbling.

8. Let the pie cool on a wire rack before serving it slightly warm with vanilla ice cream.

To Accompany or Not to Accompany— That Is the Question

How to accompany a slice of pie is a culinary preference that is very individual and sometimes very hotly debated. For example, cheese or no cheese; the ice cream goes on top or on the side; whipped cream always. Yours is the choice. In the recipes that follow we make recommendations for accompaniments to that proud wedge on a dessert plate. We stipulate either ice cream or whipped cream whenever we think the pie (or cake) will be especially enhanced by one or the other. Cheese with apple pie? . . . You are on your own!

Cheddar Crust Apple Pie

One 9-inch double-crust pie

Cheddar Dough (page 117)

6 or 7 large Granny Smith
   apples, or 3 pounds
2 tablespoons freshly squeezed
   lemon juice
1 1/4 cups sugar, plus
   additional for sprinkling on
   the top crust
1/2 cup unbleached all-purpose
   flour
3/4 teaspoon ground cinnamon
3/8 teaspoon salt
2 tablespoons unsalted butter,
   softened
Egg glaze made by beating
   together well 1 large egg and
   3 tablespoons cold water

*C*heddar cheese and apples are a tried-and-true combination and make this a wonderful pie to bake any time in the fall, but remember it, in particular, for dessert on Thanksgiving Day. It is a pie for grown-ups, though; if you've lots of young children at the table, you might want to make especially for them the Caramel Apple Pie (page 22), as sweet and homey as this pie is savory and rich. We have the French to thank for this Cheddar variation on the classic pastry crust, *pâte brisée.*

1. Peel, core, and slice the apples a generous 1/16-inch thick, which is thin but not paper thin, to make roughly 8 1/2 cups slices (see Tip). In a large bowl, toss the apple slices gently with the lemon juice.

2. In a small bowl, stir together with the wire whisk the sugar, flour, cinnamon, and salt. Add to the apple slices and toss gently to coat them evenly.

3. Preheat the oven to 425°F.

4. Divide the Cheddar dough into 2 unequal pieces, making the piece for the top crust slightly larger. On a lightly floured surface, roll the smaller piece into an 11-inch round. Line the pie plate with the bottom crust and fill it with the apples, using your hands to shape them into a firmly packed mound only slightly higher in the center than at the sides.

5. Reflour the work surface and roll the remaining pastry into an 11-inch round.

6. With a sharp paring knife, trim the edges of the bottom crust to a 1/4-inch overhang. Dot the filling with the butter. Arrange the top crust over the filling and trim the crust to no more than 3/4-inch overhang. Fold the top crust under the edge of the bottom crust and flute the edges decoratively, pressing together

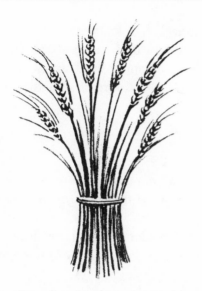

with your thumb and forefinger. (Note that this is a very flaky pastry that puffs up during baking, making it necessary to trim the edges more closely than we normally recommend elsewhere in the book.) In the center of the top crust make three 1 3/4-inch slashes in the sheaf of wheat pattern.

7. Bake the pie for 20 minutes. Reduce the oven temperature to 375°F. and continue to bake the pie for about 40 minutes, until the pastry is medium golden brown in color and the juices are bubbling.

8. Ten minutes before the end of the baking time, brush the top with egg glaze and sprinkle with sugar.

9. Let the pie cool on a wire rack before serving it slightly warm or at room temperature.

🍎 *Tip:* To slice apples thin but not paper thin, first halve, core, then peel them. Place each half, cut side down, on a cutting board. Using a sharp knife, slice the apples lengthwise to a generous 1/16-inch thickness so that each slice is translucent but not super-thin. If the apples are sliced too thin, you will loose the splendid texture of the filling and its congenial relationship to the tender, flaky crust.

Caramel Apple Pie

One 9-inch double-crust pie

Old-Fashioned Dough (page 111)

The Filling

1/2 cup dark brown sugar, firmly packed

1 1/2 tablespoons cornstarch

1 teaspoon ground cinnamon

1/4 teaspoon salt

5 1/2 tablespoons unsalted butter, melted

3/4 teaspoon pure vanilla extract

5 or 6 Golden Delicious apples, about 2 1/2 pounds

The Glaze

1 tablespoon unsalted butter, melted

2 tablespoons corn syrup, light or dark

2 tablespoons dark brown sugar

1/4 teaspoon pure vanilla extract

1/4 cup finely chopped walnuts for sprinkling on the top

Caramel Apple Pie has great appeal to kids. It earns its name mostly by appearance. The top, with its dark caramelized glaze sprinkled with walnuts, resembles a caramel- and nut-candied apple. Under the crust, the apple slices are colored and richly flavored with brown sugar.

1. Preheat the oven to 425°F.

2. Make the filling. In a small bowl, combine the brown sugar, cornstarch, cinnamon, and salt. Stir in the melted butter and vanilla. The mixture will be thick.

3. Quarter, core, and peel apples. Cut each quarter into 3 wedges. Measure the apples into a large bowl. They will make roughly 7 cups.

4. Add the sugar mixture to the apple slices, tossing gently until the slices are fairly evenly coated.

5. Line the pie plate with the bottom crust and mound the apple filling into it. Trim the bottom crust to a 1/2-inch overhang. Arrange the top crust over the filling; leave a 1-inch edge. Fold the top crust under the edge of the bottom crust and flute the edges decoratively, pressing together with your thumb and forefinger. Make 5 or 6 steam vents, each 3/4-inch long, around the center of the top crust.

6. Bake the pie for 15 minutes. Reduce the oven temperature to 350°F. and continue to bake the pie for 35 minutes.

7. While the pie is baking, make the glaze. In a small bowl, combine the melted butter, corn syrup, brown sugar, and vanilla. The mixture is thick but will thin down when applied to the hot pie.

8. Remove the pie from the oven at the end of the baking time and with a pastry brush, immediately apply the glaze to the top

Vanilla ice cream, as accompaniment

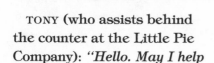

TONY (who assists behind the counter at the Little Pie Company): *"Hello. May I help you?"*

WOMAN: *"Thank you anyway. I just came in to smell."*

crust but not the fluted edges. Don't worry about applying the glaze perfectly evenly over the peaks and valleys of the bumpy pie crust (see Tip). The glaze will continue to melt and coat the pie as it finishes baking. Sprinkle the glaze with the walnuts.

9. Return the pie to the oven for 10 to 15 minutes, or until the glaze is browned and bubbling.

10. Let the pie cool on a wire rack before serving it at room temperature with a scoop of vanilla ice cream.

Tip: As you brush on the glaze, some of the pastry may flake off a bit. It is nothing to be concerned about; just continue to apply the glaze, as gently as possible, using a minimum of pressure.

Apples and Cider Pie

One 9-inch double-crust pie

Old-Fashioned Dough (page 111)

2 cups apple cider plus 1/4 cup, if needed (see Tip)

1 cup water

4 1/2 cups (9 ounces) sulfured dried apples, loosely packed into a measuring cup

4 teaspoons sugar, plus additional for sprinkling on the top crust

3/4 teaspoon ground cinnamon

1/2 teaspoon grated nutmeg

2 tablespoons unsalted butter, softened

Egg glaze made by beating together well 1 large egg and 3 tablespoons cold water

Heavy cream, as accompaniment

*N*othing fancy about this one—it's just a plain good pie, with an honestly arrived-at double-apple flavor. The slightly resistant bite of the dried apples adds interesting texture to the filling. (Another plus: Unlike very juicy fresh fruit pies, dried apple pies don't spill over onto your oven floor.)

You can make this pie over a two-day period. Mix the pastry and cook the apples on day one. Roll the pastry, mix the filling, and bake on day two. Enjoy on days two and maybe even three.

1. In a 3- to 4-quart nonaluminum saucepan over medium-high heat, bring the 2 cups cider, the water, and the dried apples to a boil. Reduce the heat and simmer about 5 minutes, stirring occasionally, until the apples are just tender. They should not be soft or mushy. Let the apples cool to room temperature in their cooking liquid. Refrigerate, covered, several hours or overnight.

2. Preheat the oven to 400°F.

3. In a small bowl, stir together with a wire whisk the sugar, cinnamon, and nutmeg.

4. If the cooked apples have absorbed all the cooking liquid, add the 1/4 cup cider. Stir in the sugar mixture.

5. Line the pie plate with the bottom crust and spoon the filling into it. Trim the bottom crust to a 1/2-inch overhang. Dot the filling with the butter. Arrange the top crust over the filling; leave a 1-inch edge. Fold the top crust under the edge of the bottom crust and flute the edges decoratively, pressing together with your thumb and forefinger. With a sharp knife, cut several 1 3/4- to 2-inch steam vents around the center of the top crust. Brush the top with egg glaze and sprinkle with sugar.

6. Bake the pie for 45 to 50 minutes, until the pastry is golden brown and the pie is puffed and steaming. (There will be no bubbling juices, as with a fresh fruit pie, to indicate doneness.)

7. Let the pie cool on a wire rack before serving it slightly warm or at room temperature with a pitcher of heavy cream as an accompaniment.

 *Tip:* If what you have on hand is apple juice, by all means use it in place of the apple cider.

Pear-Apple Crumb Pie

One 9-inch single-crust pie

Rich and Tender Dough (page 116)

THE FILLING

**3 fully ripe but still firm Anjou
    pears, about 1 1/2 pounds
3 Granny Smith apples, about
    1 1/2 pounds
2 tablespoons freshly squeezed
    lemon juice
2/3 cup sugar
2 tablespoons unbleached
    all-purpose flour
3/4 teaspoon ground cinnamon
1/8 teaspoon salt**

*T*he pleasures of a crumb-topped pie, nubbly and sweet, go all the way back to childhood. How often, then, did we ask for a slice just for its crumb topping? And when those precious crumbs would fall into our laps how fast we'd scoop them back up and into our mouths! You may have something of the same reaction to the topping on this pie. The crumbs are large, spicy, and pebbly, and the filling, a natural combination of two autumnal fruits, will fill your house with the most wonderful aroma of commingled cinnamon, apples, and sweet pears.

1. Preheat the oven to 425°F.

2. Prepare the filling. Peel the pears. Cut each in half lengthwise and remove the core and any long fibers. Cut each half crosswise into 1/8-inch slices to make roughly 4 cups. Peel, core, and halve the apples. Cut them into 1/8-inch slices, to make roughly 4 cups. In a large bowl, toss the pear and apple slices with the lemon juice.

3. In a small bowl, stir together with a wire whisk the sugar, flour, cinnamon, and salt. Add the mixture to the fruit and toss gently to coat the slices evenly.

4. Line the pie plate with the bottom crust and make a fluted edge (page 128). Spoon the filling into it, using your hands to shape it into a smooth mound that is only slightly higher in the center than it is at the sides.

5. Bake the pie for 45 minutes.

The Crumb Topping

1 cup unbleached all-purpose
  flour
1/2 cup light brown sugar,
  firmly packed
1 teaspoon grated nutmeg
1/2 teaspoon ground cinnamon
1/4 teaspoon ground mace
1/4 teaspoon salt
8 tablespoons (1 stick) cold
  unsalted butter, cut into
  1/2-inch pieces

6. While the pie is baking, prepare the crumb topping. In a medium bowl, combine the flour, brown sugar, spices, and salt. With your fingertips or with an electric mixer, cut in the cold butter until all the dry ingredients are incorporated and the mixture forms large crumbs. The topping should not come together in a ball.

7. After baking the pie for 45 minutes, remove it from the oven and let it stand on a wire rack for 5 minutes. Completely cover the filling with the crumb topping. To create a pebbly effect with the topping, pinch the crumbs together to form large and small irregularly shaped pieces.

8. Return the pie immediately to the oven and continue to bake it about 20 minutes, or until the crumbs are medium golden brown in color.

9. Let the pie cool completely on the rack before serving.

Cranberry Apple Pie

One 9-inch double-crust pie

Old-Fashioned Dough (page 111)

2 cups apple cider plus 1/4 cup, if needed

2/3 cup water

4 cups (8 ounces) sulfured dried apples, loosely packed into a measuring cup

1 1/2 cups cranberries, fresh or frozen, cut in half by hand, or chopped coarse in a food processor (page 63)

1 teaspoon grated orange peel

1/4 cup sugar, plus additional for sprinkling on the top crust

1/2 teaspoon ground cinnamon

1/4 teaspoon grated nutmeg

2 tablespoons unsalted butter, softened

Egg glaze made by beating together well 1 large egg and 3 tablespoons cold water

When we first cut out a wedge of this pie, which is a variation on Apples and Cider Pie (page 24), our immediate thought was this is what an early New England pie must have been like—practical, pleasing, and plain honest. The pie is simple, but it's pretty and tasty with its double-apple flavor.

If you've the time (and inclination), slice the cranberries in half by hand, which gives the filling a special handmade look.

1. In a 3- to 4-quart nonaluminum saucepan over medium-high heat, bring to a boil the 2 cups cider, the water, and the dried apples. Reduce the heat and simmer about 5 minutes, stirring occasionally, until the apples are just tender. They should not be soft or mushy. Let the apples cool to room temperature in their cooking liquid. Refrigerate, covered, several hours or overnight.

2. Preheat the oven to 400°F.

3. If the cooked apples have absorbed all the cooking liquid, add the 1/4 cup cider. Stir in the cranberries and orange peel.

4. In a small bowl, stir together with a wire whisk the sugar, cinnamon, and nutmeg. Stir the mixture into the fruit.

5. Line the pie plate with the bottom crust and spoon the filling into it. Trim the bottom crust to a 1/2-inch overhang. Dot the filling with the butter. Arrange the top crust over the filling; leave a 1-inch edge. Fold the top crust under the edge of the bottom crust and flute the edges decoratively, pressing together with your thumb and forefinger. With a sharp knife, cut several 1 3/4- to 2-inch steam vents around the center of the top crust. Brush the top with egg glaze and sprinkle with sugar.

6. Bake the pie for 45 to 50 minutes, until the pastry is golden brown and the pie is puffed and steaming.

Softened vanilla ice cream, as accompaniment

7. Let the pie cool on a wire rack before serving it slightly warm or at room temperature, accompanied by the softened ice cream.

You wouldn't believe what it is like at Thanksgiving. I actually start planning for it in September. Over the years, we've gotten better and better at it. There are lists posted all over and schedules taped to walls for the bakers to refer to. When you have to turn out that many fresh pies in that short a time, nothing can be left to chance. It works now, but we had to learn how to do it.

There is one funny thing, though. Because the door is opened and closed so often for the pickup of the pies, the temperature in the shop drops and it gets quite cold. So all the bakers and I wear turtlenecks and long underwear under our baker's whites. There we are standing in front of deck ovens that have been on for hours on end and we're dressed for cross-country skiing. It really is a sight. We all look a lot like the bakers in our sign.

—P.H.

Granny Smith Applesauce

Makes 1 1/4 cups

**2 or 3 Granny Smith apples, 1
generous pound, peeled and
cut into 1-inch pieces
1/4 cup water**

You can imagine on any given day around Thanksgiving the number of apple cores we have left over after a full day of baking. One year we hand-sliced 1,000 pounds of apples! True to our American, primarily Midwestern roots, we thought that there had to be a use for these cores, and indeed there is—for making applesauce. We use the cores from Granny Smith apples, which, because of the way we slice the apples, still have a bit of fruit on them. We chop the cores, add a little water to them, and cook them slowly over low heat for about an hour. We then push the mixture through a food mill to make a smooth, thick, natural no-sugar-or-spices-added applesauce, which we use in Applesauce Pumpkin Pie (page 31) and Applesauce Carrot Cake (page 146). This recipe, yielding a mere 1 1/4 cups, not even near to what we make at any one time, was developed for home use. (You will be using entire apples, peeled, not just the cores.) Feel free to double it.

1. Combine the apples and water in a 3-quart nonaluminum saucepan and cover with a lid slightly ajar. Cook over moderate heat, checking the apples and stirring them every couple of minutes until they have almost completely disintegrated. This should take about 15 minutes.

2. Cover completely and let cool.

3. Work the applesauce through a food mill or sieve into a bowl. Cover and chill until needed.

Applesauce Pumpkin Pie

One 9-inch single-crust pie

Old-Fashioned Dough (page 111)

1 1/2 cups solid pack pumpkin (not pumpkin pie filling)
1/3 cup Granny Smith Applesauce (opposite) or another thick but smooth unsweetened applesauce
3 large eggs, beaten lightly
1/2 cup dark brown sugar, firmly packed
1/4 cup granulated sugar
1 1/4 teaspoons ground cinnamon
1/2 teaspoon ground ginger
1/4 teaspoon ground cloves
1/2 teaspoon salt
1 cup evaporated milk
1 teaspoon pure vanilla extract
Sweetened whipped cream, as accompaniment

*O*ne bite of this harvest-time pie and you will recognize right off that it is not *the* traditional pumpkin pie. The flavor here is a little milder, the texture slightly smoother. The element of surprise? A small amount of applesauce added to the otherwise classic filling combination. Apples and pumpkin—they work well together. Don't forget the dollop of whipped cream.

1. Preheat the oven to 425°F.

2. In a large bowl, mix together with a wire whisk the pumpkin, applesauce, and eggs.

3. In a medium bowl, stir together the sugars, spices, and salt. Stir the sugar mixture into the pumpkin mixture. Whisk in the evaporated milk and vanilla, stirring slowly so as not to create air bubbles.

4. Line the pie plate with the bottom crust and make a high fluted edge (page 128). Pour the filling into the pastry-lined pie shell and bake for 15 minutes. Reduce the oven temperature to 350°F. and continue to bake the pie for 45 minutes, or until it tests done when a knife inserted about 1 inch from the center comes out clean.

5. Let the pie cool on a wire rack before serving at room temperature or slightly chilled with sweetened whipped cream.

Sugarless Apple Pie

One 9-inch double-crust pie

Light and Flaky Dough (page 115) or Vegetable Oil Dough (page 119) (see Tip)

6 or 7 large Golden Delicious apples, about 3 pounds
4 tablespoons freshly squeezed lemon juice
1 1/2 teaspoons grated lemon peel
3/4 teaspoon ground cinnamon
3/8 teaspoon grated nutmeg
1 tablespoon cornstarch
Pinch of salt
2 tablespoons unsalted butter, softened
2 tablespoons heavy cream

*W*e are frequently asked by customers which of our pies have no sugar or low sugar—not an easy question to answer where desserts are concerned! So we developed this sugarless apple pie. Interestingly, it is one of our earliest recipes.

What is surprising about this combination is that we did not up the amount of apples or change the type. We use a variety of apples at the Little Pie Company, but chose the Golden Delicious in this recipe because it is so naturally sweet. We did, though, favor fresh lemon juice to punch up a very refreshing taste. We don't think you will miss the sugar.

1. Quarter, core, and peel the apples. Cut each quarter into 3 wedges. Measure the apples into a large bowl. They will make roughly 8 cups.

2. Add the lemon juice and grated peel.

3. In a small bowl, stir together with a wire whisk the cinnamon, nutmeg, cornstarch, and salt. Add the mixture to the apple slices and stir gently to coat them evenly.

4. Preheat the oven to 425°F.

5. Line the pie plate with the bottom crust and mound the apple filling in it, using both hands to press the apples together into a tightly packed mound. Trim the bottom crust to a 1/2-inch overhang. Dot the filling with the butter. Arrange the top crust over the apples; leave a 1-inch edge. Fold the top crust under the edge of the bottom crust and flute the edges decoratively, pressing together with your thumb and forefinger. With a sharp knife, cut 5 or 6 steam vents, each 1/2-inch long, around the center of the top crust. With a pastry brush, brush the top, but not the edges, evenly with the heavy cream.

6. Bake the pie for 20 minutes. Reduce the oven temperature to 350°F. and continue to bake the pie for 40 to 45 minutes, until the pastry is nicely browned and the juices are bubbling.

7. Let the pie cool on a wire rack before serving it slightly warm or at room temperature.

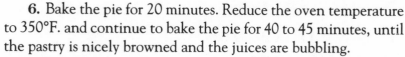 *Tip:* When made with Vegetable Oil Dough, this pie, already lower in sugar, becomes lower in cholesterol, too—more healthful, in short.

It took three months to draw the logo of the company. We wanted it to feel contemporary, but look handmade, all-American, old-time. I was a full-time illustrator then. I started with some very abstract designs, then turned to just pies and apples, then to modern drawings, and even considered plain type, with no drawing, for a while. It was clear to all of us that the two bakers were what we wanted. They are having fun, being lighthearted. We wanted them to give off that feeling, and I had learned how to do that illustrating children's books.

—M.D.

McIntosh Apple Pie with Raisins and Rum

One 9-inch double-crust pie

Old-Fashioned Dough (page 111)

1 cup dark seedless raisins, rinsed and patted dry with a towel

2/3 cup light brown sugar, firmly packed

1/3 cup dark rum

1/3 cup water

2 teaspoons freshly squeezed lemon juice

5 large McIntosh apples, about 2 1/2 pounds, firm and fresh

2 tablespoons granulated sugar

2 tablespoons cornstarch

1/2 teaspoon ground cinnamon

2 tablespoons unsalted butter, softened

2 tablespoons heavy cream for brushing on the top crust

*T*he idea for this pie came from our apple raisin bars, cookies that were on the original Little Pie Company menu and because people took to them are still on it today. For many of our apple pies we use Golden Delicious apples, but here the McIntosh combines in a particularly successful way with the rum and raisins. It is important to use "Macs" that are really firm. Try for new-crop ones.

1. In a small nonaluminum saucepan, combine the raisins, brown sugar, rum, water, and lemon juice. Bring to a simmer over medium heat. Remove the pan from the heat and let cool to room temperature.

2. Quarter, core, and peel the apples. Cut each quarter into 2 wedges to make roughly 4 cups.

3. In a small bowl, stir together with a wire whisk the granulated sugar, cornstarch, and cinnamon. In a bowl, toss the apples with the cinnamon mixture. Mix in the raisins and their liquid.

4. Preheat the oven to 425°F.

5. Line the pie plate with the bottom crust and spoon the filling into it, distributing the apples and raisins evenly. Trim the bottom crust to a 1/2-inch overhang. Dot the filling with the butter. Arrange the top crust over the filling; leave a 1-inch edge. Fold the top crust under the edge of the bottom crust and flute the edges decoratively, pressing together with your thumb and forefinger. Brush the top with the heavy cream. With a sharp knife, make five or six 3/4-inch long steam vents around the center of the top crust.

6. Bake the pie for 15 minutes. Reduce the oven temperature to 350°F. and continue to bake the pie for 45 minutes, or until the pastry is golden brown and the juices are bubbling.

7. Let the pie cool on a wire rack before serving it slightly warm or at room temperature.

Pour-Through Apple Pie

One 9-inch semi-free-form pie

A generous 1/2 recipe (see
Tips) of Old-Fashioned Dough
(page 111)

5 or 6 large Golden Delicious
apples, about 2 pounds
2/3 cup sugar, plus additional
for sprinkling on the top
1/3 cup unbleached all-purpose
flour
1/2 teaspoon ground cinnamon
1/4 teaspoon grated nutmeg
Egg glaze made by beating
together well 1 large egg and
3 tablespoons cold water
One 5-inch circle of aluminum
foil
2/3 cup heavy cream, at room
temperature

*T*his recipe did not start out as a pour-through pie. It began as
Easy Apple Pie, one that involved only one big circle of dough that
we'd top with apples, then cover with the edges of the dough. Easy.
No rolling out of another crust. No trimming or crimping the
edges. However, after the first few tries it became apparent that the
design of this pie was virtually an open invitation for a pour-
through of cream. So, off we started again.

Our cookbook assistant, Dianne, who affectionately refers to
this pie as a creamy apple dumpling, logged in a considerable number of hours helping to perfect this recipe. There were different
varieties of apples used, different creams—from homemade *crème
fraîche* to imported English double Devon—and different times for
pouring in the cream—a strategic consideration. It took us months
to arrive at the best combination, which in the end now seems so
obvious. Note that a large work surface is needed for rolling the pie
crust into a 16-inch circle.

1. Quarter, core, and peel the apples. Cut each quarter into 3
wedges. Measure the apples into a large bowl. They will make
roughly 5 1/2 cups.

2. In a small bowl, stir together with a wire whisk the sugar,
flour, cinnamon, and nutmeg.

3. Add the sugar mixture to the apples and toss gently to combine. Set aside while you roll out the dough.

4. Preheat the oven to 425°F.

5. On a large lightly floured surface, roll the dough out into a
16-inch circle. There is no need to trim away any slightly irregular
edges; they will contribute to the rustic charm of the pie.

6. Fold the dough in half to transfer it to the pie plate. Unfold
it and gently ease it into the plate. There will be a considerable

We take things one at a time. You want to be able to catch yourself. It's tempting in business to plunge ahead, but Arnold and I have a phrase—don't change lanes and don't go too fast.

—M.D.

amount of overhang. Press together or patch any tears or thin patches in the dough.

7. Fill the pastry-lined pie plate with the apples. With your hands, press and shape the apples into a low, compact mound that is only slightly higher in the center than at the sides.

8. Fold the overhang of dough up over the apples, easing it around them to distribute the folds of excess dough evenly. The dough will not completely cover the apples. There will be about a 3-inch opening on top—this is the opening for the pour-through.

9. Check the dough again for tears or thin spots where an apple is poking through and patch or reinforce as needed. Any holes in the baked pastry will allow the juices and cream to leak out and settle in the bottom of the pie plate, making the crust soggy.

10. Brush the pie crust with the egg glaze and sprinkle lightly with sugar. Fit the round of foil, dull side up, over the exposed apples in the center. The foil will help prevent the apples from drying out.

11. Bake the pie for 40 minutes. Remove the pie from the oven and carefully lift off the foil. With a paring knife, gently rearrange the topmost apples, pushing them down or further under the crust to help them bake fully. (In every baking we found that apple slices right at the top were slightly underdone.) Replace the foil.

12. Return the pie to the oven. Reduce the oven temperature to 350°F. and continue to bake the pie for 20 minutes.

13. Remove the pie from the oven and lift off the foil. Slowly pour the heavy cream through the opening in the top, tilting the pie to help the cream flow throughout the filling. If the cream appears to pool in the center, insert a paring knife into the apples to dislodge some of the slices and let the cream flow through.

14. Let the pie cool on a wire rack before serving slightly warm.

 Tips: Old-Fashioned Dough made with butter and the lard—not the vegetable shortening—is the easiest to work with for this pie. It holds up very well throughout all the rolling, folding, and handling, without breaking or tearing. A cool kitchen and/or a chilled rolling surface will also assist in keeping the dough firm and easier to handle.

Do not try to make half a recipe of dough. Make one full recipe, then divide it into two pieces, one larger than the other. From the smaller piece, remove a walnut-sized knob in the event you need to patch the crust. The remaining dough may be wrapped and frozen for use at a later date; it could be used to make little pies or given to a youngster for a dough rolling lesson.

Rhode Island Greening Apple Pie

One 9-inch double-crust pie

Old-Fashioned Dough (page 111) or Light and Flaky Dough (page 115)

7 or 8 Rhode Island greening apples, about 3 pounds
3 tablespoons unsalted butter
1 tablespoon freshly squeezed lemon juice
1/2 cup sugar
1 1/2 tablespoons cornstarch
1 teaspoon ground cinnamon
Pinch of salt
2 tablespoons heavy cream for brushing on the top crust

*A*s baking apples go, few, if any, surpass the Rhode Island greening. It is tart but sweet in flavor and superb to the bite. Fortunately for all of us, Rhode Island greenings are becoming more and more available at green markets and produce markets alike.

This is a true apple pie lover's kind of pie—a first-rate butter-imbued filling in the crust of your choice. If you want to gild the lily, by all means serve it with a slice or two of Cheddar, but we bet after the first taste of the pie you won't even want the cheese. This is another good choice for dessert on Thanksgiving.

1. Quarter, core, and peel the apples. Cut each quarter into 2 wedges. They will make roughly 7 cups.

2. In a large skillet over medium heat, melt the butter. Add the apple slices and cook them for 6 to 7 minutes, stirring gently every minute or so, until the butter has been absorbed. The slices will still be firm; they will be pale in color, not brown at all. Remove the skillet from the heat. Stir in the lemon juice. Let the mixture cool to room temperature.

3. Preheat the oven to 425°F.

4. In a small bowl, stir together with a wire whisk the sugar, cornstarch, cinnamon, and salt.

5. Add the sugar mixture to the apple slices and toss gently to coat them evenly.

6. Line the pie plate with the bottom crust and spoon the apples and their juices into it, mounding the filling slightly with your hands. Trim the bottom crust to a 1/2-inch overhang. Arrange the top crust over the filling; leave a 1-inch edge. Fold the top crust under the edge of the bottom crust and flute the edges decoratively, pressing together with your thumb and forefinger.

Brush the top crust with the heavy cream. With the tip of a sharp knife, make 5 or 6 steam vents, each 3/4-inch long, around the center of the top crust.

7. Bake the pie for 20 minutes. Reduce the oven temperature to 375°F. and continue to bake the pie for about 35 minutes, until the pastry is golden brown and the juices are bubbling.

8. Let the pie cool on a wire rack before serving it slightly warm or at room temperature.

This is years ago now, but I've been known to carry pies around in a beautiful hand-crafted pie box, with five shelves and a solid brass latch. Every day I'd go out of the apartment, using this magnificent carrier as my attaché case. The neighbors must have thought it a little odd. And unless everyone on that floor had a cold, it was impossible not to notice the smell of cinnamon and apples coming out from under my door. The building didn't say anything, though. I think they must have been getting a little suspicious when the fourth oven they had installed in my apartment broke down. By that time, luckily, we had signed a lease for our first store on 43rd Street. We renovated it and moved in as quickly as we could.

—A.W.

Blackberry Apple Pie

One 9-inch latticetop pie

Old-Fashioned Dough (page 111)

1 pound individually quick-frozen blackberries, unthawed (or fresh—the season is short), about 3 1/2 cups

1 1/2 cups diced Golden Delicious apples, 1 1/2 to 2 large apples, peeled, cored, and cut into 1/4-inch dice

2/3 cup sugar, plus additional for sprinkling on the lattice strips

2 tablespoons instant tapioca

2 tablespoons freshly squeezed lemon juice

Egg glaze made by beating together well 1 large egg and 3 tablespoons cold water

*S*ome of us remember as children asking our mothers, "Is it time yet? Is it time for blackberry picking?" Then one hot day in July it was, and we'd scramble to the patch, gingerly push the brambles aside, and pick to our hearts delight, our hands turning a striking blue from the juices. Those days are but a memory for most of us, but the enjoyment of a simple blackberry pie lives on. We bake this pie, made with a latticework top and apples, too, especially for Mother's Day.

1. In a 3- to 4-quart nonaluminum saucepan, combine the blackberries, apples, sugar, tapioca, and lemon juice and cook over medium heat for about 5 minutes, stirring often, until the berries begin to release their juice. (Most of the berries will remain whole.) Transfer the filling to a bowl, cover, and refrigerate until cold.

2. Preheat the oven to 425°F.

3. Line the pie plate with the bottom crust and pour the filling into it. For the lattice strips, roll the dough into a 13-inch circle and cut twelve 1-inch-wide strips.

4. Brush the lattice strips with the egg glaze and sprinkle them with sugar. Arrange the strips over the filling. Trim the bottom crust edge and the strips to a 1-inch overhang. Fold the bottom edge up over the lattice strips to form a thick edge, then flute the edges decoratively.

5. Bake the pie for 20 minutes. Reduce the oven temperature to 350°F. and continue to bake the pie for 35 minutes, or until the pastry is browned and the juices are bubbling.

6. Let the pie cool thoroughly on a wire rack before serving it slightly warm or at room temperature.

FRESH FRUIT PIES

Strawberry Rhubarb Pie   46

Blueberry Pie   48

Three-Berry Pie   51

Cherry Pie   54

Peach Pie   56

Peach Raspberry Pie   58

Pear Pie   59

Pears with Sambuca Pie   60

Plum Pie   62

Cranberry Raisin Pie   63

When the Little Pie Company decided to branch out and make sweets that did not always include apples, the obvious choice was to bake with other fresh fruits.

It seemed natural to follow the seasons, to use what was best in the market when it was meant to be there—no strawberry rhubarb pies in November or December or plum pies in May. We'd follow the calendar, not push the seasons, and when the berries became scarcer and scarcer, but a lingering memory of summer, we looked to the plums to carry us into fall. Only once did we agree to use fruit that was frozen and basically out of season—cherries—to celebrate George Washington's birthday. We figured that was a good enough reason! And every year since we've baked them into a splendid latticework pie.

What follows, then, are the pies that we like best, that use the best fruits of spring, summer, and fall. You will find favorite combinations: strawberry and rhubarb, raspberry, strawberry, and blueberry, for these are impossible to improve upon, so marvelous and mellow are their flavors, so lovely their looks. Several of these seasonal pies require the lattice top; the fillings simply warrant disclosure. In fact, many of these pies we make especially for the holidays—Easter and July 4th—for they are celebratory, befitting grand celebrations. An ancillary pleasure: While these fruit pies bake, your kitchen, your whole house even, will be perfumed with the essences of the bounty of nature.

BASIC EQUIPMENT

9-inch glass pie plate, deep dish (the one we use measures 1 3/4 inch deep and holds 5 cups liquid volume)
9-inch glass pie plate, standard (the one we use measures 1 1/2 inches deep and holds 4 cups liquid volume)
(Both plates were measured on the outside from the bottom to the top edge of the rim.)
Colander
Kitchen towel, one that you don't mind being colored by beautiful berry juice

NICE TO HAVE ON HAND BUT NOT ESSENTIAL

Assorted round cutters or aspic cutters (for cutouts and vents)

A General Reminder

Pies made with fresh fruit are juicy, and more often than not will require your attention 10 to 15 minutes before the end of the baking time to monitor the state of their bubbling juices. Heed the size of flute suggested in the recipes, as this is our way, too, of keeping those flavorful juices in the pie where they belong.

Why Tapioca?

At the Little Pie Company we use instant tapioca to thicken the fillings of many of our fruit pies, which tend to be very juicy. Flour can also be used, as can cornstarch, and some people even opt for arrowroot. We quite often use tapioca, though, because it lends a homey, jellylike consistency to the filling and keeps the fruit juices clear and vibrant in color.

Instant, or quick-cooking, tapioca is available at most supermarkets in eight-ounce boxes. If you are devoted to fruit pies you will find the box disappearing very quickly.

Strawberry Rhubarb Pie

One 9-inch latticetop pie

Old-Fashioned Dough (page 111) or Light and Flaky Dough (page 115)

2/3 cup sugar, plus additional for sprinkling on the lattice strips

2 tablespoons plus 1 teaspoon instant tapioca

1/2 teaspoon ground cinnamon

1 1/2 cups halved hulled fresh strawberries

4 cups pink or red sliced fresh rhubarb, each slice 1/2 inch thick

Egg glaze made by beating together well 1 large egg and 3 tablespoons cold water

*T*o many people rhubarb, like asparagus and soft-shelled crabs, means spring. We fall into that group with this spring pie, which is a simple combination of the best of the season—rhubarb and strawberries. We have lattice-worked the top because the color of the filling is simply too beautiful not to be seen. And because it is a kind of celebration pie, make it especially for family and friends.

1. In a small bowl, stir together with a wire whisk the sugar, tapioca, and cinnamon. Sprinkle the mixture over the strawberries and rhubarb and gently stir it in. Let the fruit filling stand for 15 minutes.

2. Line the pie plate with the bottom crust and spoon in the filling, mounding it gently in the center.

3. Preheat the oven to 425°F.

4. For the lattice top, on a lightly floured surface, roll the dough into a 13-inch circle and cut eight 1 1/2-inch strips. With a pastry brush, brush the strips with the egg glaze and sprinkle them with sugar. Arrange the strips over the filling. Trim the bottom crust edge and the strips to a 1-inch overhang. Fold the bottom edge up over the strips to form a thick edge, then flute the edges decoratively, pressing together with your thumb and forefinger.

A Longing

WOMAN (with gusto and delight, after eyeing the window and spotting strawberry rhubarb pie): *"Oh, how wonderful! I've been waiting months for this pie."*

5. Bake the pie for 20 minutes. Reduce the oven temperature to 375°F. and continue to bake the pie for 40 to 45 minutes, until the pastry is well browned.

6. Let the pie cool on a wire rack before serving it slightly warm or at room temperature.

The Pleasure of Fresh Rhubarb

If you are lucky enough to have a stand of fresh rhubarb in your backyard, remember when you go to pick it that only the stalks are edible; the leaves, which contain oxalic acid, are highly toxic and must be discarded. Rhubarb, known in New England as long ago as the eighteenth century, where it was called "pie plant," freezes well. It can also be held wrapped in a damp towel inside a plastic bag for at least five days in the refrigerator.

When we were kids in North Dakota, my brothers and sisters and I—there were seven of us—used to go out in the spring to our rhubarb patch. We carried little bowls of sugar. We'd pick the stalks, lick the ends, then dip the stalks into the sugar.

My mom each year would use the rhubarb to put up strawberry rhubarb sauce. Jars and jars of it. When we were testing our strawberry rhubarb pie, it was important to me that it have the flavor of her sauce.

—M.D.

Blueberry Pie

One 9-inch double-crust pie

Old-Fashioned Dough (page 111)

5 cups fresh blueberries or two 12-ounce packages individually quick-frozen blueberries

2/3 cup sugar, plus additional for sprinkling on the top crust

2 1/2 tablespoons instant tapioca

3/8 teaspoon ground cinnamon

2 teaspoons freshly squeezed lemon juice

2 tablespoons unsalted butter, softened

Egg glaze made by beating together well 1 large egg and 3 tablespoons cold water

*E*ach year, at the end of June, Arnold, master of window dressing at the Little Pie Company, puts up the July 4th window. His display, a collection of charming painted and weathered wooden pieces of Americana that includes, among many other whimsical things, a lady teetering on a tightrope, puts all of us in a silly, happy, summer vacation kind of mood. It is as if the circus of Americana has come to the Little Pie Company. And each year we feature a pie for July 4th, which sits plunk down in the middle of the circus! It's this one: a two-crusted blueberry winner decorated, patriotically, with a circle of tiny star-shaped cutouts on the top crust. Try it with another American specialty—softened vanilla ice cream.

1. If fresh blueberries are used, remove underripe berries, leaves, and any pieces of stem. Quickly rinse the berries in a colander and shake off the excess water. Gently pat the berries dry with a clean kitchen towel. Place the berries in a large mixing bowl.

If frozen berries are used, place them in a large mixing bowl and allow them to thaw partially, to the point where they have softened but not yet begun to juice.

2. In a small bowl, stir together with a wire whisk the sugar, tapioca, and cinnamon.

3. Add the sugar mixture and the lemon juice to the blueberries and toss lightly to combine. Let the mixture stand for 15 minutes.

4. Preheat the oven to 425°F.

5. Line the pie plate with the bottom crust and spoon the blueberries and all their juices into it, mounding them so that they are slightly higher in the center than on the sides. Dot the filling with the butter.

6. The top crust may be designed in one of two styles, either simply, with plain steam vents, or with the star cutout–type steam vents, which we use. For the simple look, arrange the top crust over the blueberries. Trim the edges of the pastry, leaving a 1-inch overhang on both top and bottom crusts. Press the top and bottom edges of pastry together and fold them under to form a thick and high edge. Flute the edges decoratively, pressing together with your thumb and forefinger. This is a juicy pie and the substantial fluted edges will help keep the juices within the pie. Make several 1 1/2-inch steam vents near the center of the top.

To make star-shaped vents, roll out the top crust. Use a star-shaped aspic cutter or a tiny cookie cutter 3/4 to 1 inch in size. Press the star cutter into the dough, being careful not to cut completely through the dough. The "star" should remain partially attached so it won't fall out when the dough is lifted and transferred to cover the filling. Make a circle of 6 or 7 stars around the center of the dough and press a single star in the middle. Carefully transfer the crust to cover the filling. (If any of the stars fall out, simply put

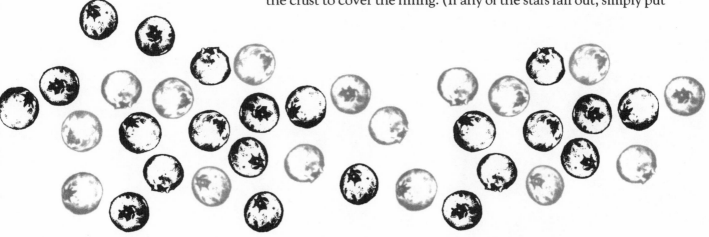

them back in their spaces.) Trim the edges of the pastry, leaving a 1-inch overhang on both top and bottom crusts. Press and flute the edges as described above.

7. Bake fresh blueberry pie for 15 minutes. Reduce the oven temperature to 375°F. and continue to bake the pie for about 35 minutes, until the juices are bubbling in the center and the pastry is browned. Ten minutes before the end of the baking time, brush the top crust with the egg glaze and sprinkle it with sugar.

Bake a pie made with frozen berries for 25 minutes, then reduce the oven temperature to 375°F. and bake it for about 35 minutes, or until the juices are bubbling in the center and the pastry is browned. Ten minutes before the end of the baking time, glaze and sprinkle the top with sugar as described above.

8. Let the pie cool completely on a wire rack before serving.

Three-Berry Pie

*One 9-inch deep-dish pie, lattice
or plain double-crust top*

**Old-Fashioned Dough (page
111)**

**3/4 cup sugar, plus additional
for sprinkling on the top crust**
1/4 cup cornstarch
1/2 teaspoon ground cinnamon
**1 1/2 cups hulled strawberries,
fresh or individually quick
frozen, halved (if using frozen
berries, partially thaw them
before halving)**
**2 1/2 cups blueberries, fresh or
quick frozen**
**2 cups raspberries, fresh or
quick frozen**
**Egg glaze made by beating
together well 1 large egg and
3 tablespoons cold water**

*Y*ou can make this pie, so plump and full of strawberries, blueberries, and raspberries, with either a lattice or plain top.
The lattice version is showy and highlights the gemlike color of
the combined berry juices, which as the pie bakes bubble up over
the edges of the strips (and onto the oven floor).

The plain top, covered version makes for a more toned-down
presentation, but the crust does have a purpose, helping to retain
the precious juices inside the pie, keeping it plump and juicy. The
decision is yours; either way, a deep-dish pie plate is a must, as is a
stellar luncheon or dinner beforehand to set the stage for a dessert
filled with the flavors of summer.

1. In a large bowl, stir together with a wire whisk the sugar,
cornstarch, and cinnamon. Add the strawberries and blueberries
and toss until they are coated evenly. (If using frozen berries, let
the mixture stand until the berries are partially thawed and render
their juices.) Add the raspberries, stirring very gently to combine.

2. Preheat the oven to 425°F.

3. Line a 9-inch deep-dish pie plate with the bottom crust,
leaving a 1-inch overhang.

4. Spoon the filling into the pastry-lined pie shell.

5. For the plain double-crust pie, roll out the top crust on a
lightly floured work surface into a 13-inch circle. Cut a 1 1/2-inch
circle out of the center with a sharp paring knife or a cookie cutter.
Then make 5 or 6 cuts, each 1 inch long, radiating from the circle.
Arrange the top crust over the filling and trim the edges, being sure
to leave a 1-inch overhang. Press the top and bottom edges of the
crusts together and fold them under to form a thick and high edge.
(This will help retain the berry juices.) Flute the edges decora-

tively, pressing together with your thumb and forefinger. Brush the top crust with the egg glaze and sprinkle with sugar.

For the latticetop pie, roll the dough into a 13-inch circle and cut eight 1 1/2-inch-wide strips. Brush the lattice strips with the egg glaze and sprinkle them with sugar before separating them. Arrange the strips over the filling. Trim the bottom crust edge and the strips to a 1-inch overhang. Fold the bottom crust edge up over the lattice strips to form a thick, high edge. (This will help to retain the berry juices.) Flute the edges decoratively, pressing together with your thumb and forefinger.

For both the latticetop and double-crust pie, have a piece of aluminum foil ready. Set it on the oven floor to catch the juices only when it appears they are about to boil over, you will need to pay attention.

6. Bake the pie made with fresh fruit at 425°F. for 15 minutes. Reduce the oven temperature to 375°F. and continue to bake for 40 minutes more, or until the pastry is browned and the juices are bubbling in the middle of the pie.

Bake the pie made with frozen fruit at 425°F. for 25 minutes. Reduce the oven temperature to 375°F. and continue to bake for 50 minutes more. If necessary, during the baking of this pie, you may need to place strips of aluminum foil or a foil frame, shiny side up, around the edges of the pie to prevent overbrowning.

7. Let the pie cool completely on a wire rack before serving.

A Counter Dialogue

WOMAN: *"We'll have a small three-berry pie. To share, please."*

MAN (looking stricken): *"Do we have to?"*

Thoughts on Three-Berry Pie

Nothing beats berries from your own bushes for this pie, but top-quality individually frozen berries make an excellent substitute for a year-round three-berry pie. Should you have access to lavish amounts of fresh berries, be sure to put some by, premeasured first, in the freezer.

We tried very hard with this recipe to keep the pie as juicy as it should be, by which we mean retain its heavenly, deep red-purple juices inside the pie and off the oven floor. You will still have to check this pie as it bakes, particularly the last 15 minutes; the latticetop version is especially likely to bubble over.

Vanilla ice cream or even thick heavy cream makes a very good accompaniment.

Cherry Pie

One 9-inch deep-dish latticetop pie

Old-Fashioned Dough (page
   111)

6 cups individually quick-frozen
   pitted Montmorency cherries,
   1 pound 12 ounces
1 1/8 cups sugar, plus
   additional for sprinkling on
   the lattice strips
1/4 cup instant tapioca
1 teaspoon freshly squeezed
   lemon juice
Egg glaze made by beating
   together well 1 large egg and
   3 tablespoons cold water
Vanilla ice cream, as
   accompaniment, if desired

*T*his is a big, fat, deep-dish pie, just loaded with Montmorency cherries—the tart, almost translucent, bright red ones—which, during cherry season, we order twice weekly from an orchard in the Hudson Valley in upstate New York. Come February, when we make this pie again, for George Washington's birthday, we use frozen fruit from the same supplier. You'll see that we have called for frozen cherries below because this pie is so good it shouldn't be limited to any one season. Of course, if you can get fresh cherries, by all means use them. Again, this is a simple, particularly pretty pie, dependent upon cups and cups of good fruit. We especially like it served with vanilla ice cream on the side.

1. In a large bowl, combine the frozen cherries and sugar. Let stand until the cherries are thawed, stirring gently every once in a while. Drain the cherries in a colander, reserving the juice. There will be about 1 1/4 cups juice. Note: Check the thawed fruit for whole or partial cherry pits. Discard them.

2. In a small nonaluminum saucepan, stir together the reserved juice and the tapioca and let stand for 5 minutes. Then, over medium heat, stirring frequently, bring the mixture to a full boil. Remove the pan from the heat. Stir in the lemon juice.

3. In a large mixing bowl, pour the hot cherry juice mixture over the cherries and gently stir them together. Cover the bowl and refrigerate until thoroughly chilled, about 2 hours.

4. Preheat the oven to 425°F.

5. Line the pie plate with the bottom crust and pour the filling into it (see Tip).

6. For the lattice top, on a lightly floured surface, roll out the dough into a 13-inch circle and cut twelve 1-inch-wide lattice strips. Brush the lattice strips with the egg glaze and sprinkle them

with sugar. Arrange the strips over the filling. Trim the bottom crust edge and the strips to a 1-inch overhang. Fold the bottom crust edge up over the lattice strips to form a thick edge, then flute the edges decoratively, pressing together with your thumb and forefinger.

7. Bake the pie for 20 minutes. Reduce the oven temperature to 350°F. and continue to bake the pie for an additional 40 minutes, or until the pastry is browned and the juices are bubbling.

8. Let the pie cool completely on a wire rack before serving it at room temperature, with vanilla ice cream on the side, if desired.

Tip: Your deep-dish pie plate should have a 5-cup liquid capacity. If you don't have such a pie plate, make the pie in a 9-inch plate, but remove about 3/4 cup of the filling. In a bowl, combine the remaining filling with a splash of brandy or Cherry Heering and use as a sauce over ice cream.

A Reminder

When to accompany a slice of pie is entirely up to you. As in earlier sections, we suggest ice cream or whipped cream as an accompaniment in the following recipes when we feel it particularly suitable—as an enhancement, never as a recourse. Please use your own discretion.

Peach Pie

One 9-inch latticetop pie

Old-Fashioned Dough (page 111)

1 cup sugar, plus additional for sprinkling on the lattice strips

2 tablespoons plus 1 teaspoon instant tapioca

1/2 teaspoon ground cinnamon

7 or 8 large peaches, or 2 3/4 pounds perfectly ripe freestone-type peaches

2 teaspoons freshly squeezed lemon juice

Egg glaze made by beating together well 1 large egg and 3 tablespoons cold water

Vanilla or peach ice cream, as accompaniment, if desired

*M*ake this pie when peach season is in full swing—August or September—and the peaches are large ripe, plentiful, and at their peak flavor and best price. The golden and yellow tones of this baked pie—golden dark lattice and peachy yellow filling—suggest that the essence of summer sun has been baked right into the pie. We recommend a freestone peach, such as Elberta.

1. In a small bowl, stir together with a wire whisk the sugar, tapioca, and cinnamon.

2. Peel (page 57), halve, and pit the peaches. Cut each half into 4 slices. Measure them into a large bowl. You should have roughly 5 1/2 cups slices. Add the lemon juice and sugar mixture to the slices. Combine gently and let stand for 15 minutes.

3. Preheat the oven to 425°F.

4. Line the pie plate with the bottom crust and pour the filling into it.

5. For the lattice top, on a lightly floured surface, roll out the dough into a 13-inch circle and cut eight 1 1/2-inch-wide lattice strips. Brush the strips with the egg glaze and sprinkle them with sugar. Arrange the strips over the filling. Trim the bottom crust edge and the strips to a 1-inch overhang. Fold the bottom edge up over the strips to form a thick edge. Flute the edges decoratively, pressing together with your thumb and forefinger.

6. Bake the pie for 20 minutes. Reduce the oven temperature to 350°F. and continue to bake the pie for 40 minutes, or until the pastry is browned and the juices are bubbling.

7. Let the pie cool completely on a wire rack before serving it at room temperature, with vanilla or peach ice cream on the side, if desired.

To Peel Peaches

You will need a large (6- to 8-quart) pot of boiling water and a bowl of very cold water. Using a large serving spoon, lower the peaches, one at a time, into the boiling water. Let them stand in the water for 30 seconds to 1 minute. Then carefully remove the peaches to the bowl of cold water. Let the peaches cool briefly, remove, and with a paring knife, peel off the fuzzy skin, starting at the stem end. The skin should slip off easily. Cut each peach in half vertically and remove the pit. Slice the peaches as directed in the recipe.

Peach Raspberry Pie

One 9-inch latticetop pie

Old-Fashioned Dough (page 111)

3/4 cup sugar, plus additional for sprinkling on the lattice strips
2 tablespoons plus 1 teaspoon instant tapioca
1/2 teaspoon ground cinnamon
5 large peaches, or 1 1/2 pounds perfectly ripe freestone-type peaches
1 1/2 teaspoons freshly squeezed lemon juice
2 cups red raspberries, fresh or individually quick frozen (do not thaw frozen berries)
Egg glaze made by beating together well 1 large egg and 3 tablespoons cold water
Vanilla ice cream, as accompaniment, if desired

*T*his is a dressed-up version of the preceding recipe and undoubtedly summer's prettiest combination of colors. The bonus for the delicate and sometimes scratchy business of picking raspberries is popping a warm berry or two into your mouth before heading back to the kitchen with a basket brimming with the fragile treasures.

1. In a small bowl, stir together with a wire whisk the sugar, tapioca, and cinnamon.

2. Peel (page 57), halve, and pit the peaches. Cut each half into 4 slices. Measure them into a large bowl. You should have roughly 3 1/2 cups slices.

3. Add the lemon juice, sugar mixture, and raspberries to the peach slices. Combine gently and let stand for 15 minutes.

4. Preheat the oven to 425°F.

5. Line the pie plate with the bottom crust and pour the filling into it.

6. For the lattice top, on a lightly floured surface, roll out the dough into a 13-inch circle and cut eight 1 1/2-inch-wide lattice strips. Brush the strips with the egg glaze and sprinkle them with sugar. Arrange the strips over the filling. Trim the bottom crust edge and the strips to a 1-inch overhang. Fold the bottom edge up over the strips to form a thick edge. Flute the edges decoratively, pressing together with your thumb and forefinger.

7. Bake the pie for 20 minutes. Reduce the oven temperature to 350°F. and continue to bake the pie for 40 to 45 minutes, or until the pastry is browned and the juices are bubbling.

8. Let the pie cool completely on a wire rack before serving it at room temperature, with vanilla ice cream on the side, if desired.

Pear Pie

One 9-inch double-crust pie

Rich and Tender Dough (page 116)

7 or 8 ripe but not mushy Anjou pears, 3 1/2 pounds
1/2 cup sugar
1/4 cup cornstarch
1/2 teaspoon ground mace
1/2 teaspoon ground cinnamon
2 tablespoons unsalted butter, softened
2 tablespoons heavy cream for brushing on the top crust

An exceptionally tender pastry and mild spicing let the pears shine through in this big juicy pie. This is what we think of as a farm pie, simple and sweet: just two crusts, a few flavorings, and lots of fruit.

1. Peel the pears. Cut each in half lengthwise and remove the core and any long fibers. Cut each half into 4 lengthwise slices. Cut the long slices in half to make large chunks. Put the pear pieces in a large mixing bowl.

2. In a small bowl, stir together with a wire whisk the sugar, cornstarch, mace, and cinnamon. Add the mixture to the pears and toss gently to coat them evenly.

3. Preheat the oven to 425°F.

4. Line the pie plate with the bottom crust and turn the filling into it. Trim the bottom crust to a 1/2-inch overhang. Dot the filling with the butter. Arrange the top crust over the filling; leave a 1-inch edge. Fold the top crust under the edge of the bottom crust and flute the edges decoratively, pressing together with your thumb and forefinger. Brush the top with the heavy cream. With a sharp knife, make 5 or 6 steam vents, each 3/4 inch long, in the center of the top of the crust.

5. Bake the pie for 15 minutes. Reduce the oven temperature to 375°F. and continue to bake the pie for 50 minutes, or until the juices are bubbling and the pastry is golden.

6. Let the pie cool completely on a wire rack before serving.

Pears with Sambuca Pie

One 9-inch double-crust pie

Rich and Tender Dough (page 116)

6 ripe but firm Anjou pears, about 3 pounds in all
1 tablespoon Sambuca, or other anise-flavored liqueur
1 1/2 teaspoons freshly squeezed lemon juice
2 teaspoons grated lemon peel
2/3 cup sugar
1/4 cup cornstarch
2 tablespoons unsalted butter, softened

THE GLAZE

1/2 cup sifted confectioners' sugar
2 teaspoons freshly squeezed lemon juice
1 teaspoon Sambuca, or other anise-flavored liqueur

*A*rnold knew just how wonderful the combination of fresh pears and the flavor of licorice can be, and so we tried it in a pie. You'll find the top crust here has a surprising look, iced, as it is, with a glaze that complements and enhances the hint of the licorice flavor in the otherwise very simple pear filling. This is a good winter dessert, when pears are at their best.

1. Peel the pears. Cut each in half lengthwise and remove the core and any long fibers. Cut each half into 4 lengthwise slices. Cut the long slices in half to make large chunks. Put the pear pieces in a large mixing bowl and toss them gently with the Sambuca, lemon juice, and lemon peel.

2. In a small bowl, stir together with a wire whisk the sugar and cornstarch. Add the mixture to the pears and stir gently to combine.

3. Preheat the oven to 425°F.

4. Line the pie plate with the bottom crust and turn the fruit into it. Trim the bottom crust to a 1/2-inch overhang. Dot the filling with the butter. Arrange the top crust over the filling. Leave a 1-inch edge. Fold the top crust under the edge of the bottom crust and flute the edges decoratively, pressing together with your thumb and forefinger. With the tip of a sharp knife, make 5 or 6 steam vents, each 3/4-inch long, around the center of the top crust.

5. Bake the pie for 15 minutes. Reduce the oven temperature to 375°F. and continue to bake the pie for 50 minutes, or until the pastry is golden brown and the juices are bubbling.

6. While the pie is baking, make the glaze. Put the confectioners' sugar in a small bowl. Stir in the lemon juice and Sambuca.

I was in a master's program at the University of Minnesota in educational psychology and many of the courses I took had to do with how people learn. Problem solving and analyzing are not random; they are systematic. You can learn how to do them. When I taught, I applied those principles in the classroom. I brought them with me here, too.

—M.D.

The glaze will be very thick but will become soft and spreadable when spread on the hot pie.

7. Remove the pie from the oven and while it is still hot apply the glaze, using either a spatula or the back of a spoon. Cover the top crust entirely with the glaze.

8. Let the pie cool on a wire rack before serving it at room temperature.

I got some very good advice when I was a sophomore in high school. A wonderful drama and speech coach of mine told me to leave my hometown and pursue other things in life. I didn't know what he meant at the time, but it brought me to New York, where my career as an actor got started.

New York is my home. I love this city. My idea of a good time is to walk—anywhere, everywhere. There's everything you could possibly want to see in New York City.

—A.W.

Plum Pie

One 9-inch double-crust pie

Old-Fashioned Dough (page 111)

9 to 11 dark red-skinned plums, about 2 1/4 pounds
2 teaspoons freshly squeezed lemon juice
1 cup sugar, plus additional for sprinkling on the top crust
3 tablespoons instant tapioca
1 teaspoon ground cinnamon
3 tablespoons unsalted butter, softened
Egg glaze made by beating together well 1 large egg and 3 tablespoons cold water

The Perfect Plum

Ripe plums will be slightly soft at the stem end; if they are soft and slightly sticky, they are overripe. Should the plums you buy need additional ripening, let them stand at room temperature for a day or two.

If color were the only criterion, this pie would be our favorite for looks alone. The plum-red baked fruit is gorgeous. Begin looking for the red-skinned Santa Rosa plums as summer draws to a close, choosing ripe, deeply colored fruit. Do not use Italian prunes, which are small, dark, purple plums somewhat oval in shape. This pie is very, very good served with a scoop or two of vanilla ice cream.

1. Preheat the oven to 425°F.

2. Halve and pit the plums. Cut each half into 4 wedges. Measure them into a large bowl. They will make roughly 7 1/2 cups. Toss the plums with the lemon juice.

3. In a small bowl, stir together with a wire whisk the sugar, tapioca, and cinnamon. Add the mixture to the plums and stir gently to coat the fruit. Let stand for 15 minutes.

4. Line the pie plate with the bottom crust and mound the filling into it. Trim the bottom crust to a 1/2-inch overhang. Dot the filling with the butter. Arrange the top crust over the filling. Fold the top crust under the edge of the bottom crust and flute the edges decoratively, pressing together with your thumb and forefinger. With the tip of a sharp knife, make 5 or 6 steam vents, each 3/4-inch long, around the center of the top crust.

5. Bake the pie for 15 minutes. Reduce the oven temperature to 375°F. and continue to bake the pie for 50 to 55 minutes more, until the juices are bubbling and the pastry is golden brown. Ten minutes before the end of the baking time, brush the top crust with the egg glaze and sprinkle with sugar.

6. Let the pie cool thoroughly on a wire rack before serving.

Cranberry Raisin Pie

One 9-inch double-crust pie

Old-Fashioned Dough (page 111) or Vegetable Oil Dough (page 119)

One 12-ounce bag whole cranberries, either fresh or frozen (about 3 cups), halved or coarsely chopped (see Tip)

1 cup dark seedless raisins, coarsely chopped

1 cup sugar

2 tablespoons all-purpose flour

1/2 teaspoon ground ginger

1/8 teaspoon salt

2 tablespoons unsalted butter, softened

2 tablespoons heavy cream for brushing on the top crust

The touch of ground ginger in this recipe sets the cranberries off to their best advantage. This pie is perfect for the fall or winter and particularly good for Thanksgiving. You will find the taste rich and fruity; a small wedge should satisfy.

1. Combine the chopped cranberries and raisins in a large mixing bowl.

2. In a small bowl, stir together with a wire whisk the sugar, flour, ginger, and salt. Add the sugar mixture to the fruit and stir to combine.

3. Preheat the oven to 425°F.

4. Line the pie plate with the bottom crust and turn the filling into it. Trim the bottom crust to a 1/2-inch overhang. Dot the filling with the butter. Arrange the top crust over the filling; leave a 1-inch edge. Fold the top crust under the edge of the bottom crust and flute the edges decoratively, pressing together with your thumb and forefinger. Brush the top crust with the heavy cream. With a sharp knife, make several 1 1/2-inch steam vents in the center of the top of the crust. (This is a juicy filling and if the vents are too small the top crust may split while baking.)

5. Bake the pie for 15 minutes. Reduce the oven temperature to 350°F. and continue to bake the pie for 45 minutes, or until the pastry is golden and the juices are bubbling.

6. Let the pie cool on a wire rack before serving it slightly warm or at room temperature.

Tip: If you use the food processor to chop the cranberries, stop processing before all of them are completely chopped. Simply cut the last few whole ones in half with a knife. If you wait until all the berries are fully chopped, most of them will be minced—not the right texture for this pie.

CREAM, CURD, AND CUSTARD PIES

Banana Cream Coconut Pie   70

Chocolate Cream Pie   72
  WHIPPED CREAM   74

Key Lime Pie   76

Lemon Meringue Pie   78

Custard Pie   80

Coconut Custard Pie   82

Buttermilk Pie   84

$\mathscr{C}$ream, curd, and custard pies have pleasing, comforting, and nurturing qualities that reach right back to our earliest memories. Indeed, these old-fashioned pies remind us of other, simpler times, when a surfeit of milk and cream and eggs had to be used up on any given farm on any given day across America. Most of us buy these ingredients now, and, thankfully, they are still plentiful. So are the pleasures of these soothing pies.

The cream pies that follow are rich, inviting, and appropriately creamy. The curd pies speak for themselves with their tangy flavors and light textures. Lastly, the custard pies are eggy and silky, the kind that slide right down as they should.

As to the crusts for these special pies, both cream pies, the Lemon Meringue, and the Key Lime require a fully baked shell. You will find the directions for preparing one on page 133. In effect, these simple pies are made even simpler because they *must* be done in stages. The custard pies require lightly baked shells, the directions for which you will find in the recipes, and only one dough, the Vegetable Oil (page 119), can we recommend for its keeping properties.

It is no accident that early on in the life of the Little Pie Com-

A Primer: How Do They Differ?

Cream pies have milk and/or cream, egg, sugar, and cornstarch-based fillings that are cooked and poured into baked pie shells.

Curd pies—and we use the term loosely here to apply to Lemon Meringue Pie and Key Lime Pie—have a filling that usually includes citrus juice, egg yolks, sugar, and sometimes cornstarch. These are cooked until thickened but not boiled, and poured into baked pie shells. Classic curds are used as spreads on scones or lightly toasted breads. A well-made curd should be smooth; you should never detect any cooked egg yolk in it.

Custard pies have milk and/or cream, egg, and sugar-based fillings that are poured into pie shells that are either baked or unbaked. The pies are then baked in the oven.

pany we decided to offer these specific pies. Most of them are American classics, and, as you will discover after baking them, a carefully made one is hard to forget.

BASIC EQUIPMENT

9-inch glass pie plate
Heavy-bottomed saucepan (especially for combining and cooking the fillings for cream pies)
Double boiler (for melting chocolate)
Sieve
4-sided box grater
Medium whisk
Electric mixer (for making meringues)

NICE TO HAVE ON HAND BUT NOT ESSENTIAL

Pastry bag fitted with number 30 star tip

The Return of the Glass Milk Bottle

There was a wonderful sound as we were growing up and it came with the whir of the milk truck drawing up to the stoop. The engine would grind down to a groan, then the milkman would jump down with a clink—his glass bottles tapping against the metal carrier. We had left our empty bottles out to be picked up and as he transferred the full bottles out and the empty ones into the basket, the glass clinked over and over again. It was a bell-like, sweet sound, memorable like the milk he was delivering that was fresh from the dairy.

Something happened, though—progress—and glass milk bottles gave way to cardboard cartons and plastic containers. You'd see milk being transported in tanker trucks. For all anyone knew milk came from a well. And the milk tasted different. There was none of that lovely cream that collected on the top of the glass bottle, right underneath the paper plug that served as a cap.

Apparently others regretted the disappearance of the glass milk bottle, too, because we're seeing it again, and it is just as lovely as it once was. There aren't many of them; it is an expensive business, glass bottling, but the milk in glass bottles we've seen reads NO HORMONES, NO ANTIBIOTICS. Even the cows are different. So is the milk. The cream is back. And those bottles, they are the real old-fashioned ones, with the dairy logo actually processed into the glass the way it used to be. There is a dollar deposit to ensure the return of each of the bottles, which seems reasonable. We've come back to glass.

Banana Cream Coconut Pie

One 9-inch pie

Light and Flaky Dough (page 115) or Vegetable Oil Dough (page 119)

1/2 cup sugar
4 tablespoons cornstarch
1/2 teaspoon salt
4 egg yolks, lightly beaten
2 1/2 cups cold milk
2 tablespoons unsalted butter
2 1/2 teaspoons pure vanilla extract
1 cup sweetened flaked coconut (see Tips)
2 large, just-ripe bananas
Sweetened whipped cream, as accompaniment, if desired

$\mathcal{I}$t seemed natural to us to combine the best of a banana cream pie with the pleasure of a coconut cream one. People love cream pies; we think it must have something to do with how basic, sweet, and easygoing they are. Built from the bottom up, this cream pie starts with a crisp-flaky crust that is topped with slices of ripe bananas, a smooth vanilla pudding with lots of sweetened coconut mixed in, then a sprinkling of more coconut, this time toasted to a crunch.

1. Make a 9-inch fully baked pie shell with a fluted edge as directed on page 133.

2. In a heavy-bottomed saucepan off the heat, stir the sugar, cornstarch, and salt until well blended.

3. In a medium bowl, stir together the egg yolks and milk and add them to the sugar mixture; stir until combined, then scrape the bottom and sides of the pan with a rubber spatula to make sure that every last bit of sugar is mixed in.

4. Cook the mixture over medium heat, stirring constantly, until it thickens and boils. Reduce the heat to medium-low and continue to cook the pudding, stirring, for 1 minute.

5. Remove the pan from the heat and stir in the butter and vanilla until blended.

6. Gently mix in 3/4 cup sweetened coconut. Place a piece of wax paper or plastic wrap directly on the surface of the filling as a cover to prevent a skin from forming. Let the filling cool for about 30 minutes.

7. Preheat the oven to 350°F.

8. Spread the remaining 1/4 cup sweetened coconut on a cookie sheet and bake it for 10 to 12 minutes, stirring several times, until it is toasted a medium golden brown.

*It may be that I was
predestined to be a pie man.
As a child, I had a great time
making pies with mud.*

—*A.W.*

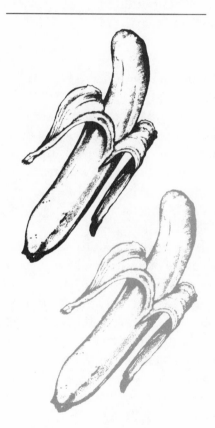

9. Slice the bananas 1/4-inch thick and arrange them over the bottom of the prebaked shell. Spoon the filling over the bananas and smooth it with the back of a spoon. Sprinkle the toasted coconut over the filling.

10. Let the pie cool to room temperature. Then refrigerate until thoroughly chilled, about 2 hours. Cover only after the pie is thoroughly chilled.

11. Serve with sweetened whipped cream on the side, if desired.

Tips: Shredded fresh coconut, used in Coconut Custard Pie (page 82) and Coconut Cake (page 166), is not recommended here. You want the additional sweetness of the commercially prepared coconut.

If you'd rather not use the grated coconut in the filling, by all means leave it out, but you may then want to try the vanilla filling with the Pecan Coconut Crust (page 121).

This pie is best served the day it is made. On the second day, the bananas will begin to darken, and by the third day the crust will be a shadow of its former self as well.

Chocolate Cream Pie

One 9-inch pie

Light and Flaky Dough (page 115), Vegetable Oil Dough (page 119), or Pecan Coconut Crust (page 121)

THE CHOCOLATE CREAM FILLING

3 ounces unsweetened chocolate

3/4 cup plus 2 tablespoons sugar

4 1/2 tablespoons cornstarch

1/2 teaspoon salt

3 egg yolks, lightly beaten

2 3/4 cups milk

1/4 cup heavy cream

1 1/2 teaspoons pure vanilla extract

1 tablespoon unsalted butter

THE GARNISH

3/4 cup chilled heavy cream

2 teaspoons superfine sugar

*W*e happen to know that the filling for this pie doesn't always make it into the shell: Sometimes the desire for warm chocolate pudding served in a puddle of cool cream is so overpowering that the crust becomes an afterthought! Chocoholics, in particular, will like the flavor—it's only sweet enough. And should the chocolate cream and pastry eventually team up, chill the pie first, then slather it with sweetened whipped cream (page 74).

1. Make a 9-inch fully baked pie shell with fluted edge as directed on page 133.

2. Make the chocolate cream filling. Melt the chocolate in a microwave oven or uncovered in the top of a double boiler set over hot—not boiling—water, stirring frequently. Remove the top from the bottom of the boiler when the chocolate is melted.

3. In a heavy-bottomed saucepan off the heat, stir together the sugar, cornstarch, and salt until well blended.

4. In a medium bowl, stir together the egg yolks, milk, and cream and add them to the sugar mixture. Stir until combined, then scrape the bottom and sides of the pan with a rubber spatula to make sure that every last bit of sugar is mixed in.

5. Cook the mixture over medium heat, stirring constantly, until it thickens and boils. Reduce the heat to medium-low and continue to cook the pudding, stirring, for 1 minute.

6. Remove the pan from the heat and stir in the melted chocolate, vanilla, and butter. Place a piece of wax paper or plastic wrap directly on the surface of the filling as a cover to prevent a skin from forming. Let the filling cool for about 30 minutes.

7. Stir the cooled filling and pour it into the prebaked shell. Once again, place a cover directly on the surface of the filling. Let

the pie cool to room temperature, then refrigerate it until thoroughly cooled, about 2 hours.

8. Prepare the garnish. In a chilled bowl with an electric mixer or by hand, beat the heavy cream and sugar until stiff peaks form.

9. Remove the cover from the pie and spread the whipped cream over the top. Or fill a pastry bag fitted with a number 30 star tip and pipe a border of rosettes around the rim.

🍎 *Tips:* The chocolate filling makes a really good pudding on its own. Serve warm with a pitcher of heavy cream.

If you make this pie with the Pecan Coconut Crust, do not flute the edge on the shell. Do, however, flute the edges if you are using either of the other two suggested doughs.

Whipped Cream

THE FOOD PROCESSOR
METHOD

About 1 1/3 cups

1 cup heavy cream, chilled
2 1/2 teaspoons superfine sugar

*T*he Little Pie Company has a candy-apple red counter with seven matching stools, from some of which you can watch the pies being made. The service at the counter is uncomplicated and friendly. There are beverages—coffee, tea, milk, apple cider, or bottled water—and slices of cake, or cookies, bars, or muffins, or the daily specials, or, of course, pie—either the little five-inch ones or by the slice—served plain, with Bassetts French Vanilla Ice Cream, or our own whipped cream.

We make a dense and smooth whipped cream. It looks almost like softened vanilla ice cream, not airy or fluffy at all, and to achieve that richer consistency we make it in a food processor fitted with the steel blade with cream that has 40 percent butterfat. Most heavy creams on the market these days have 36 percent butterfat, have been ultra-pasteurized, and have had stabilizers added (which change the taste). This cream will whip up just fine, but does not hold up for long without becoming watery.

Look for heavy cream with 40 percent butterfat in gourmet food shops, or if you are lucky ask for it at your local dairy or at one of its outlets. The difference when whipped is dramatic.

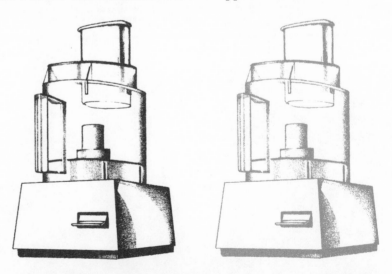

I did a lot of cooking as a child, but desserts were what I liked making best.

—*P.H.*

1. Chill the food processor bowl and the steel chopping blade.

2. Pour the chilled cream into the processor bowl fitted with the steel blade and add the sugar.

3. Process for 45 seconds. Scrape down the sides and bottom of the bowl and continue to process, stopping the machine every 10 seconds to check the cream and scrape the bowl, until the cream is smoothly beaten to a dense and creamy consistency.

4. Use the cream immediately or store it in a tightly covered container in the refrigerator. It will keep well for 24 hours. After that it will begin to deflate but may be rebeaten in the processor with success.

Key Lime Pie

One 9-inch pie

Light and Flaky Dough (page 115)

4 egg yolks, stirred with a fork
1 14-ounce can sweetened condensed milk
1/2 teaspoon finely grated lemon or lime peel
1/2 cup plus 2 tablespoons lime juice (see Tips)
1 cup heavy cream, chilled
1 tablespoon superfine sugar

*E*very year in March we hold our "Pick the Winners of the Academy Awards" contest. Customers fill out ballots, circling the nominees they think will win in each of sixteen categories. The prize for the top score is a dessert from us, pick-up-able at another time. On the night of the Oscars, lots of Key lime pies are carted out of the store. In any event, this is a celebration pie—sweet, tangy, and superbly American. Use good lime juice. Traditionally, Key limes are used in this pie, but the number grown is small so they are not usually available to most of us. And be sure to remember this classic pie year round; it's particularly pleasing, rich but refreshing as it is, in summer.

1. Make a 9-inch fully baked pie shell with fluted edge as directed on page 133.
2. Preheat the oven to 350°F.
3. In a medium mixing bowl, stir together the egg yolks, condensed milk, and lemon or lime peel. Slowly stir in the lime juice. Pour the filling into the prebaked shell.
4. Bake the pie for 20 minutes.
5. Let the pie cool completely on a wire rack. Refrigerate the pie for about 2 hours, or until thoroughly chilled.
6. In a chilled mixing bowl, beat the heavy cream with the sugar until it holds stiff peaks. Spoon the whipped cream or pipe rosettes of it with a pastry bag fitted with a number 30 star tip around the edges of the filling. Serve at once.

Tips: The juice we use to make this pie is called Nellie and Joe's Key Lime Juice and it is bottled in Key West, Florida. It has a good, authentic flavor that bakes into a good, authentic pie.

Arnold and I share a real interest in, you could call it a love for, diners. We wanted to start one, in fact. A diner is simple, basic, American, and the food, in a good one, can be great. We opened the Little Pie Company instead. It's no accident, though, that there is a counter and stools here.

—M.D.

You will have 4 egg whites left over after making this pie. If you like, whip up a meringue with them. Follow the directions for making meringue on page 78, swirl it over the lime filling here, and brown it as instructed on page 79 for Lemon Meringue Pie. While not the classic version of Key Lime Pie, it is awfully good.

Don't be concerned about the small gap between the filling and the crust in the finished pie. The filling is so rich even a thin layer pleases. Simply cover the gap with whipped cream.

Lemon Meringue Pie

One 9-inch pie

Light and Flaky Dough (page 115)

5 tablespoons cornstarch
1 cup sugar
1/4 teaspoon salt
1 3/4 cups cold water
4 large eggs, separated (reserve whites for meringue)
1/2 cup plus 2 tablespoons freshly squeezed lemon juice
2 teaspoons grated lemon peel
3 tablespoons unsalted butter

THE MERINGUE

4 large egg whites (reserved from above)
1/4 teaspoon cream of tartar
Pinch of salt
1/2 cup superfine sugar
3/4 teaspoon pure vanilla extract

What is it about lemon meringue pie that makes it so beloved? For some, it is the tart, puckery, marvelous lemon filling; for others, it is that super, sort-of fifties two-tone look. For still others, it is that splendid marriage of sweet and sour, smooth and grainy. For us, it is all of those, and then some—one of America's grandest pies. This version is high-standing and proud.

1. Make a 9-inch fully baked pie shell with fluted edge as directed on page 133.

2. In a heavy-bottomed nonaluminum saucepan, combine the cornstarch, sugar, and salt. Stir in the cold water. Place the saucepan over medium heat and, stirring constantly, bring to a boil. Boil, stirring, for 1 minute.

3. In a bowl, whisk half the hot sugar mixture into the egg yolks. When thoroughly combined, stir the mixture into the saucepan. Bring the yolk mixture to a gentle boil and, stirring constantly, cook for 2 minutes.

4. Remove the pan from the heat and add the lemon juice and peel and butter. Stir until the butter is melted and fully incorporated. Allow the filling to cool slightly while you make the meringue.

5. Preheat the oven to 350°F.

6. In a large bowl (not a plastic one), beat the egg whites, cream of tartar, and salt with an electric mixer on low speed until foamy. Increase the speed to high and beat the whites until soft peaks begin to form. Gradually beat in the sugar, about 1 tablespoon at a time, and continue to beat the whites until stiff, glossy peaks form. Beat in the vanilla.

7. Pour the lemon filling into the prebaked shell. Using a large spoon, pile the meringue on top of the filling, mounding it higher

in the center and spreading it out to the edges of the pastry. Make sure there are no gaps. For a pretty presentation, use the back of the spoon to create swirls and peaks and valleys in the meringue.

8. Bake the pie for 12 to 15 minutes, until the top is lightly golden brown. (The "peaks," of course, will be darker.)

9. Let the pie cool on a wire rack to room temperature before serving it—in large slices. Refrigerate the pie unless it is to be served directly after it has reached room temperature. Remove from the refrigerator about 10 minutes before serving. The pie is best served cold but not just out of the refrigerator.

Tips: Let the egg whites come to room temperature just before making the meringue. A quick way of doing it is to place the bowl of whites over a bowl of warm water and stir them gently for a few minutes to take off the chill.

Don't let the fun of working with meringue get the better of you. If you make the peaks too high, they will burn.

This pie is best eaten the day it is made. Store it, if you must, refrigerated and wrapped in plastic wrap with toothpicks pushed into the meringue to prevent the film from resting directly on the meringue. Store 2 days. Kept longer than that, the meringue will begin to "weep," meaning that the sugar is starting to liquefy, a natural occurrence that does not affect the taste but does alter the appearance.

Custard Pie

One 9-inch pie

Vegetable Oil Dough (page 119)

2 cups milk
1 cup heavy cream
4 large eggs plus 1 egg yolk
1/2 cup sugar
1 1/2 teaspoons pure vanilla
   extract
3/8 teaspoon salt
1/2 teaspoon grated nutmeg

𝒲ere it not for America's deep rural roots and the number of farms stretching from one coast to the other, custard might not have achieved the popularity it did as this country was aborning. But fields and grass and cows and chickens and eggs were plentiful at one time, and custard was made frequently in farm kitchens across this land. It was an easy dessert, recognized for being exactly what it still is—nourishing to the body and comforting to the spirit, something both children and grown-ups could like. Though other things changed, custard held on, outlasting other fancier desserts. It was only a matter of time until it was used as the filling in a pie.

This is one of those old-time custard pies, eggy, soothing, and sweet. It is simple and slips right down in just the right way. Don't try to use another dough here. The vegetable oil pastry holds its shape beautifully while baking and remains crisp while other crusts turn soggy much sooner. This one even holds up during refrigeration. Note that the shell is fully baked beforehand but is removed from the oven about 2 minutes earlier than a fully baked vegetable oil pastry shell for a precooked filling such as the chocolate cream. The fluted edges of the pastry will be only a very pale brown but will finish browning as the custard bakes. Note that the same shell prebaking procedure is used for making the crust for Coconut Custard Pie (page 82), should something a little more exotic (we mean more than the flavor of custard and nutmeg!) strike your fancy, and for the Buttermilk Pie (page 84).

1. Preheat the oven to 425°F.

2. On a lightly floured surface, roll out the dough into a circle to fit a 9-inch pie plate, preferably made of glass. Ease the dough into the plate and flute the edges (see page 128). Reserve any

leftover dough. With the tines of a fork, very lightly prick the bottom and sides of the shell, making tiny holes that will close up during baking. Bake the shell for 6 or 7 minutes. Remove the shell from the oven and with the fork lightly prick the dough anywhere it has puffed up. Return the shell to the oven and bake for 8 minutes, until just very lightly browned. Remove the shell to a wire rack to cool completely. Use the leftover dough to patch any small holes or cracks. (If you have used a glass pie plate, they are easy to find: Just hold the plate up to the light.)

3. Make the filling. In a saucepan, combine the milk and the cream and heat over medium heat until small bubbles form around the edges of the pan. Remove the pan from the heat.

4. In a medium bowl, beat the whole eggs and yolk with a wire whisk until combined. Stir in the sugar, vanilla, and salt. Slowly stir in the warm milk mixture, being careful not to mix so fast as to create bubbles.

5. Strain the mixture through a sieve into the baked shell. This step is best done as close to the oven as possible. It is difficult to move the filled shell without sloshing the filling over the edges of the pastry.

6. Sprinkle the filling with the nutmeg. Bake the pie for 15 minutes. Reduce the oven temperature to 350°F. and continue to bake the pie for 20 to 25 minutes, or until the custard tests done when a knife inserted 1 1/2 inches from the outer edges comes out clean. The filling will still be soft in the center but will finish baking as it cools. If the pie is baked until the center is fully cooked and firm, the custard will be overcooked and watery.

7. Let the pie cool thoroughly on a wire rack. Then refrigerate it for several hours before serving. Remove the pie from the refrigerator a few minutes before serving to take the chill off.

Coconut Custard Pie

One 9-inch pie

Vegetable Oil Dough (page 119)

2 1/3 cups milk
3 large eggs plus 1 egg yolk
1/2 cup sugar
1 teaspoon pure vanilla extract
1/4 teaspoon salt
1 cup finely shredded fresh
   coconut (page 83), lightly
   packed, about 2 1/4 ounces,
   or unsweetened desiccated
   coconut from a health food
   store
Lightly sweetened whipped
   cream, as accompaniment, if
   desired

*T*his pie and Coconut Cake (page 166) both call for grated fresh coconut, and one day we were really awed by an employee at the Little Pie Company when he took a coconut in one hand and a hammer in the other and proceeded to rotate the coconut as he whacked it with the hammer. Fortunately there was a bowl nearby, because in a matter of seconds, he was draining the cracked coconut over the bowl. Then, with a few more hits, he had neatly shelled the coconut. The amazing part of it was that even though the meat was cracked it was still in one piece! And it had taken, literally, only a minute or so to do.

The texture of this tender and silky baked custard filling is heightened by the shredded fresh coconut added to it.

1. Prepare a 9-inch lightly baked pie shell with fluted edge as directed on pages 80–81.

2. Preheat the oven to 425°F.

3. In a saucepan, heat the milk over medium heat until small bubbles form around the edges of the pan.

4. In a medium bowl, beat the eggs and yolk with a wire whisk just until they are combined. Stir in the sugar, vanilla, and salt.

5. Slowly stir in the warm milk, being careful not to create bubbles. With a spoon or rubber spatula, stir in the shredded coconut. At a work space near the stove, pour the filling into the pie shell.

6. Bake the pie for 15 minutes. Reduce the oven temperature to 350°F. and continue to bake the pie for about 20 minutes, or until the filling tests done. The center will be only softly set; a clean knife inserted 1 1/2 inches from the outer edges should come out clean.

A fresh coconut should feel heavy for its size and you should be able to hear the liquid sloshing around inside of it. Check around each of the three eyes that there is neither moisture nor mold.

7. Let the pie cool to room temperature on a wire rack. Then refrigerate it for several hours. Remove the pie shortly before serving to take some of the chill off. If desired, serve with lightly sweetened whipped cream.

To Shred Fresh Coconut

Unlike the baker at the Little Pie Company who can shell a fresh coconut, in one piece no less, in less than 2 minutes, most of the rest of us need directions. This is how the rest of us do it, and you can, too.

1. With an awl or a nail and hammer, pierce the three dark eyes in the coconut.

2. Drain the liquid into a bowl. If desired, strain and refrigerate it for later use in beverages. Know that this watery liquid is not "coconut milk," though, which is made from grated coconut meat that has steeped in water or milk.

3. Bake the drained coconut in a preheated 375°F. oven for 15 minutes.

4. Wrap the coconut in an old, clean towel, place it on a sturdy work surface, and with the hammer, break it into large pieces.

5. With a blunt knife, separate the white meat from the shell. Then using a vegetable peeler, pare away the dark skin.

6. Rinse the pieces of coconut under running water and pat dry.

7. Shred the coconut in a food processor fitted with a fine shredding disk or by hand with a grater.

Buttermilk Pie

One 9-inch pie

Vegetable Oil Dough (page 119)

THE BUTTERMILK FILLING

3/4 cup plus 2 tablespoons
    sugar
1/4 cup unbleached all-purpose
    flour
1/4 teaspoon grated nutmeg
1/4 teaspoon salt
4 large eggs, separated (reserve
    the whites for making the
    meringue)
2 cups buttermilk, at room
    temperature
2 tablespoons Cointreau

THE MERINGUE

4 large egg whites (reserved
    from above)
1/4 teaspoon cream of tartar
Pinch of salt
1/2 cup superfine sugar
3/4 teaspoon pure vanilla
    extract

*S*ome of us remember being taken as children in the summer to the state fair and watching as our parents on one of those hot and dusty days drank down big, tall glasses of buttermilk. They did it with real relish. We found it sort of strange that anyone, especially our parents, would like milk with butter in it. We didn't think much more about it, though, as long as we didn't have to drink it.

We now know buttermilk doesn't have butter in it. We also know that it is tangy and wonderfully refreshing as a pie filling, especially at the end of a spicy meal or during one of those state fair–type sultry days. Even though this is an old-fashioned pie, we've availed ourselves of a modern-day convenience—the food processor—which combines the filling in a flash. Lastly, this pie is topped with swirls of lightly baked meringue. This is an easy pie to make, and just as easy to like.

1. Make a 9-inch lightly baked pie shell with fluted edge as directed on pages 80–81.

2. Preheat the oven to 425°F.

3. Make the filling. In the bowl of a food processor fitted with the steel blade, process the sugar, flour, nutmeg, and salt until combined.

4. Add the egg yolks, buttermilk, and Cointreau and process for about 10 seconds to combine. Scrape down the sides of the bowl with a rubber spatula and process again for a few seconds. Pour the filling into the baked shell.

5. Bake the pie for 15 minutes. Reduce the oven temperature to 350°F. and bake the pie for an additional 25 to 30 minutes, until the filling is slightly puffed at the edges and beginning to crack, and the center of the pie holds firm when the pie is gently shaken (see Tips).

6. Let the pie cool on a wire rack for a few minutes while you prepare the meringue.

7. In a large bowl (not a plastic one), beat the egg whites, cream of tartar, and salt with an electric mixer until foamy. Increase the speed to high and beat the whites until soft peaks begin to form. Gradually beat in the sugar, about 1 tablespoon at a time, and continue to beat the whites until stiff, glossy peaks form. Beat in the vanilla.

8. Using a large spoon, pile the meringue on top of the baked filling, mounding it higher in the center and spreading it out to the edges of the pastry. Make sure there are no gaps. For a pretty presentation, use the back of the spoon to create swirls and peaks and valleys in the meringue.

9. Bake the pie for 12 to 15 minutes, until the top is lightly golden brown. (The "peaks" of course, will be darker.)

10. Let the pie cool on the rack to room temperature. Then chill for about 3 hours before serving.

Tips: Let the egg whites come to room temperature just before making the meringue. A quick way of doing it is to place the bowl of whites over a bowl of warm water and stir them gently for a few minutes to take off the chill.

Don't insert a knife into the filling to test for doneness. Unlike custard pies made with milk and cream, this pie is a soft, creamy one. The knife will be coated with filling even though the custard is done.

And More Favorite Pies

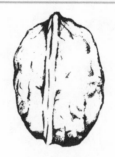

*A*fter collecting our most favorite apple pie, fresh fruit pie, and cream and custard pie recipes, you would have thought that that would have done it—there were no more favorite pies to be included. But, as we soon realized, there were, and they constitute a grouping of not only our favorites, but other people's as well.

It was Arnold who encouraged our efforts in perfecting a peanut butter pie with chocolate-covered walnut crust. Arnold especially likes nuts—note that there are two different kinds in the pie. And it was Arnold also who urged us on to find a wonderful walnut pie. He wanted to combine walnuts with maple syrup, but we ended up with finely ground walnuts and two cups of heavy cream, one of the most luxurious fillings you may ever taste.

Everyone's idea of favorite is different, but in the recipes that follow there is a slice to please everyone. Moreover, these are pleasant pies to bake—some easy, others a little more challenging.

BASIC EQUIPMENT

You probably have all the baking equipment needed to make the pies in this section of favorites. You will need a food processor, though, for combining and chopping some of the ingredients in the fillings.

I'm a people person. That's why I stopped working as an illustrator. It's too lonely. Meeting customers is what I like, building a bridge. Some of them have been coming for a long time. We've gotten to know each other. That's the way it used to be in a small town. That's the feeling we wanted to create here.

We ask them if they'd like to try a new product we are working on or sample a variation on something. People like that. They like to be involved. In turn, it's been customers who have given us many of the posters and pictures on the walls. That's very meaningful to us.

—M.D.

Southern Pecan Pie

One 9-inch single-crust pie

Rich and Tender Dough (page 116)

3 large eggs
1 cup light Karo (corn) syrup
1 teaspoon pure vanilla extract
1/3 cup light brown sugar, firmly packed
1/3 cup granulated sugar
2 1/2 tablespoons unsalted butter, melted and cooled
Pinch of salt
2 cups pecan halves
1 cup chilled heavy cream, whipped, as accompaniment, if desired

*P*ecan pie requires a not-so-simple balancing act to keep it sweet but not cloying. We wanted a pie loaded with pecans, caramel in flavor but not overly so, rich and pleasing but not sugary. Judging from the number of these pies we sell each year at Thanksgiving and Christmas, we think we found the formula.

This is definitely a special occasion pie, but one that shouldn't be limited to just the holidays. It deserves the freshest pecans available. (If you buy them in bulk, store them airtight in the freezer.) Serve pecan pie with unsweetened whipped cream.

1. Preheat the oven to 350°F.

2. Line a pie plate with the bottom crust and make a fluted edge (see page 128).

3. In a large bowl, lightly beat the eggs. Stir in the Karo syrup and vanilla.

4. In a small bowl, combine the two sugars, making sure that there are no lumps.

5. Add the sugars, the melted butter, and the salt to the syrup mixture, stirring to combine.

6. Spread the pecans evenly over the bottom of the shell and pour the filling over them.

7. Bake the pie for 55 to 60 minutes, or until the filling is slightly puffed up and a knife inserted about 1 1/2 inches from the center comes out clean.

8. Let the pie cool on a wire rack before serving at room temperature, with unsweetened whipped cream, if desired.

Kentucky Sweet Potato Pie

One 9-inch single-crust pie

Rich and Tender Dough (page 116)

2 cups mashed sweet potatoes, about 1 1/2 pounds sweet potatoes, baked, peeled, and mashed with the back of a fork, with small lumps remaining

3/4 cup half-and-half or light cream

1 teaspoon pure vanilla extract

4 tablespoons (1/2 stick) unsalted butter, softened

1/2 cup light brown sugar, firmly packed

2 large eggs

3/4 teaspoon ground cinnamon

1/2 teaspoon ground mace

1/4 teaspoon ground cloves

1/4 teaspoon ground ginger

1/4 teaspoon salt

*A*round Thanksgiving at the Little Pie Company we've been known to bake forty pounds of sweet potatoes at one time and peel all of those by hand, too! We suspect that you won't be needing quite that many potatoes, but you will need to know the difference between a sweet potato and a yam, which even the supermarket can muddle up. Sweet potatoes are long and slender in shape, and have a deep orange-colored skin and a lovely orangey flesh. Yams are members of a different family, are considerably larger in size and lighter in color. Sweet potatoes, like regular white potatoes, are very good baked, and equally good when used for pies.

This is a rich, spicy pie, with an intentionally lumpy filling, clearly made by hand, the old-fashioned way. We've called it Kentucky sweet potato pie because it's like one, we imagine, that might have been served for dessert in many a porticoed home in that bluegrass state over the holidays. The reputation of sweet potato pie grew, though, and now the pleasures of this lovely orange-hued filling are enjoyed coast to coast.

1. Preheat the oven to 350°F.

2. In a large bowl, combine the mashed sweet potatoes with the half-and-half and vanilla.

3. In a medium bowl, cream together the butter and sugar until fluffy. Beat in the eggs, one at a time.

4. Stir the egg mixture into the sweet potato mixture.

5. Combine all the spices and salt in a small bowl and stir them well into the filling.

6. Line a pie plate with the bottom crust and make a fluted edge (see page 128). Pour the filling into it, spreading it into an even layer with a spatula. Make a decorative zigzag or swirl pattern on the top.

*For the first two years,
Thanksgiving meant thirty-six
hours of working round the
clock. We actually took the
phone off the hook! We were
sold out, and we couldn't have
baked another pie if we'd tried.
We've gotten better organized
since then, but no less busy.*

—P.H.

7. Bake the pie for 1 hour, until very lightly browned and slightly puffed in the middle.

8. Let the pie cool on a rack before serving it slightly warm or at room temperature.

Street Life, or A Day in the Life of the Little Pie Company

Scene: Bakers rolling out dough in the kitchen; pies being cooled near the open screen door; a full display of large and little pies in the window, the aroma of apples and cinnamon and butter wafting downwind, perfuming the sidewalk . . .

WALK-IN: *"Say, do you know where I could get a good apple pie around here?"*

Peanut Butter and Chocolate Pie

One 9-inch single-crust pie

The Pastry

1/2 cup walnut pieces

1/2 cup unbleached all-purpose flour

1/4 cup light brown sugar, firmly packed

3 tablespoons cold unsalted butter, cut into 1/2-inch pieces

The Chocolate Layer

8 tablespoons (1 stick) unsalted butter, cut into 1/2-inch pieces

4 ounces semisweet or bittersweet chocolate, broken into pieces

1 1/2 tablespoons strongly brewed coffee

*E*ach of us has different tastes when it comes to pies. This one, especially favored by Arnold, is popular with all of us, though. It's a scrumptious, rich peanut butter mousse over a layer of smooth chocolate that coats crisp walnut pastry. The beauty of this multi-stepped special-occasion dessert, aside from its combination of some of America's favorite flavors, is that there are several places where it is possible to stop and freeze or refrigerate the pie and then continue at a later, more convenient time. The finished pie can also be frozen, a big asset.

1. Prepare the pastry. In a food processor fitted with the steel blade, process the walnut pieces until finely chopped but not ground. Add the flour and brown sugar and process to combine, scraping down the bowl with a rubber spatula as needed. Add the butter and process until the dough forms large crumbs, but do not let it come together into a ball.

2. Press the pastry over the bottom and up the sides of a 9-inch pie plate, forming about a 1/4-inch smooth ridge along the top edge of the crust. Refrigerate about 30 minutes or freeze until firm.

3. Preheat the oven to 350°F.

4. Bake the shell about 25 minutes, until lightly browned and set. Let cool on a wire rack.

5. Prepare the chocolate layer. Combine the butter, chocolate, and coffee in a small pot or mixing bowl. Place over hot but not boiling water and stir constantly until the chocolate and butter are melted. Pour all but about 2 tablespoons of the chocolate mixture into the bottom of the cooled shell. (The reserved chocolate will be used later on for garnish.) Refrigerate for about 1 hour or freeze until firm.

THE PEANUT BUTTER MOUSSE

1/4 cup plus 2 tablespoons (3 ounces) cream cheese, at room temperature

2/3 cup sifted confectioners' sugar

3/4 cup old-fashioned–style smooth peanut butter, with no sugar added (if unsalted, add 1/8 teaspoon salt to recipe; see Tips)

1/3 cup milk

1 teaspoon pure vanilla extract

1 cup heavy cream

2 tablespoons chopped peanuts for garnish (optional)

6. Make the peanut butter mousse. In a food processor fitted with the steel blade, process the cream cheese, confectioners' sugar, and peanut butter until smooth. With the machine running, add the milk, vanilla, and salt, if needed, and process until smooth and well blended. Transfer to a large bowl.

7. In a chilled bowl, whip the cream with a wire whisk or a hand-held electric mixer until stiff peaks form. Fold the cream into the peanut butter mixture to make a smooth mousse. Spoon the mousse over the chocolate layer in the shell and smooth the top with a spatula. If desired, sprinkle the chopped peanuts over the top of the mousse.

8. Warm the reserved chocolate until it is melted. Either drizzle it free-form from a teaspoon, or fill a small plastic zip-top sandwich bag and clip off a tiny corner of the bag to make a pinhead-size hole, or use a paper cone and decoratively pipe it over the top of the pie.

9. Chill the finished pie for at least 4 hours before serving or freeze it. Thaw overnight in the refrigerator.

Tips: Old-fashioned peanut butter is ground roasted peanuts with no sugar or emulsifiers added. Check the label to see if salt has been added. Oil will float to the top of this kind of butter, but all you need to do is stir it back in.

For peanut butter lovers, this mousse makes a wonderful dessert as is, topped, if you like, with a little whipped cream and a sprinkling of crushed peanuts.

Pineapple-Apricot Crumb Pie

One 9-inch single-crust pie

Light and Flaky Dough (page 115)

THE FILLING

11 ounces (about 1 3/4 cups) pitted dried sulfured apricots, cut in half
2 cups cold water
One 20-ounce can crushed pineapple in natural juice
2 tablespoons freshly squeezed lemon juice
1/4 cup sugar
2 tablespoons unbleached all-purpose flour
1/8 teaspoon salt

THE TOPPING

3/4 cup unbleached all-purpose flour
3/4 cup sugar
1/2 teaspoon ground ginger
1/8 teaspoon salt
6 tablespoons cold unsalted butter, cut into small pieces

This pie came into being very simply—Arnold wanted an apricot pie! We began with fresh apricots, but, as it happened, they went out of season while we were still working on the recipe. Realities like that seem to occur frequently in the world of baking. Hence we used the next best thing—dried apricots, which combine very successfully with pineapple. The crunchy crumb topping, charged as it is with a little ground ginger, tops everything off to a tee. And who can resist the pleasures of a crumb topping? This is a good pie for winter, when sweet, sunny fruits are what you hunger for. You may even have the two main ingredients in your larder.

1. Make the filling. In a 1-quart nonaluminum saucepan, bring the dried apricots and water to a boil. Simmer, uncovered, for about 30 minutes, or until the apricots are just tender and most of the water has been absorbed. Transfer the apricots and their liquid to a large bowl and allow to cool.

2. Preheat the oven to 425°F.

3. Add the crushed pineapple with its juice and the lemon juice to the apricots.

4. In a small bowl, stir together with a wire whisk the sugar, flour, and salt. Stir the mixture into the fruit mixture.

5. Line the pie plate with the bottom crust and make a fluted edge (see page 128). Pour the filling into it.

6. Bake the pie for 15 minutes. Reduce the oven temperature to 350°F. and continue to bake the pie for 30 minutes more.

7. While the pie is baking, prepare the crumb topping. In a medium mixing bowl, combine the flour, sugar, ginger, and salt. Cut the butter in using your fingertips to form crumbs the size of tiny peas. Refrigerate until needed.

8. Remove the pie from the oven and increase the oven temperature to 450°F.

9. Allow the pie to stand for about 10 minutes while the oven heats up. Then top the still-warm pie with the crumb topping. (Use as much of the topping as desired; depending upon your tastes, you may want to use all or only part of it. Whatever is leftover cannot be reused.) Bake for 15 to 20 minutes, until the crumbs are nicely browned.

10. Let the pie cool on a wire rack before serving it slightly warm or at room temperature.

Date Walnut Pie

One 9-inch single-crust pie

Rich and Tender Dough (page 116)

2 large eggs
1/3 cup light brown sugar, firmly packed
1/3 cup granulated sugar
1 tablespoon unbleached all-purpose flour
1/4 teaspoon salt
1 cup heavy cream
1 teaspoon pure vanilla extract
1 cup chopped pitted dates, about 8 ounces, lightly packed in measuring cup
3/4 cup coarsely chopped walnuts
Unsweetened whipped cream, as accompaniment, if desired

*P*ull out your best china, pour a cup of coffee or tea, spoon a soft cloud of unsweetened whipped cream next to a slender slice of this rich pie—and enjoy! When the very picky Little Pie Company bakers quickly polished off the first samples of this and then asked when there would be more, we knew we had a winner.

1. Preheat the oven to 350°F.

2. Line a pie plate with the bottom crust and make a fluted edge (see page 128).

3. In a medium bowl, beat the eggs with a wire whisk until they are light and foamy. Add both the sugars, the flour, and the salt and whisk until thoroughly combined. Stir in the cream and vanilla. Add the dates and walnuts, stirring to break up any clumps of dates. Pour the filling into the shell.

4. Bake the pie for 45 to 50 minutes, until the top is golden brown and the filling is set.

5. Let the pie cool on a rack before serving it at room temperature, with unsweetened whipped cream, if desired.

   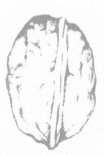 

One-of-a-Kind Walnut Pie

One 9-inch single-crust pie

Light and Flaky Dough (page 115) or Rich and Tender Dough (page 116)

4 egg yolks

2 cups heavy cream

1 1/2 cups sugar

3 tablespoons unsalted butter, melted

2 teaspoons pure vanilla extract

1/2 teaspoon salt

1 3/4 cups very finely chopped walnuts, about 7 ounces (see Tip)

10 to 12 walnut halves for garnish (optional)

*A*rnold likes sweet, creamy nut pies, and when we first went looking for a walnut pie recipe we were really in search of one made with maple syrup and nuts. As you can see from the combination below, maple syrup, good as it is, never made it into the filling, but no matter—cups of heavy cream and exceptionally finely ground walnuts did. This is a unique, rich pie, one that would be splendid for tea or for dessert during the winter months. Be sure to serve it with strong, aromatic coffee.

1. Preheat the oven to 350°F.

2. In a large bowl, beat the egg yolks lightly. Stir in the cream and add the sugar, melted butter, vanilla, and salt. Stir in the ground walnuts and combine the filling well.

3. Line the pie plate with the bottom crust and make a fluted edge (see page 128). Pour the filling into the unbaked shell and, if desired, garnish the top by "floating" the walnut halves in a decorative pattern on the surface (see Tips).

4. Bake the pie for about 1 hour and 10 minutes, or until the filling is puffed in the middle and lightly browned in color.

5. Let the pie cool completely on a wire rack before serving it at room temperature, in slender slices, with strong coffee as an accompaniment.

Tips: Chop the walnuts in a food processor fitted with the steel blade until ground, but do not let the nuts go that extra step and become pasty and oily.

To "float" walnuts halves for garnish on the filling, just lay them decoratively on the surface. If you push them into the filling, they will sink. They add a little something extra to what is otherwise a simple-looking, but not tasting, pie.

Bean Pie

One 9-inch single-crust pie

Light and Flaky Dough (page 115) or Vegetable Oil Dough (page 119)

2 1/2 cups drained cooked dried small white beans or navy beans (see On Preparing Dried Beans, opposite)
2 large eggs, lightly beaten
2/3 cup sugar
2 tablespoons unsulfured light molasses
1 1/2 teaspoons ground cinnamon
1/2 teaspoon grated nutmeg
1/2 teaspoon salt
1 teaspoon pure vanilla extract
1 1/4 cups heavy cream or evaporated skimmed milk

*T*he abiding interest that the Little Pie Company has in the traditions of wonderful American pies took Patricia one day to Reading Terminal, Philadelphia's extraordinary food, produce, flower, and so-many-other-items market right in the city. It was there that she saw a pie made with beans. That was all we needed, and after a lot of research and quite some testing of recipes, here's the pie. Like pumpkin pie, but a little heavier, Bean Pie is a very good choice for fall or winter.

We tried something a little different with it, too. Evaporated skimmed milk may be used as a substitute for the heavy cream. And if you use vegetable oil dough, which is lower in cholesterol than light and flaky dough, you lower the counts on both fat and cholesterol—no mean achievement for a dessert pie!

1. Preheat the oven to 425°F.
2. Mash the beans either by hand or in the food processor. By hand, arrange the drained cooked beans on a flat-surfaced plate—a pie plate is excellent for this—and mash them thoroughly with the back of a fork until they have the consistency of a thick paste. Scrape the paste into a large bowl.
3. In a medium bowl, stir together the beaten eggs, sugar, molasses, cinnamon, nutmeg, salt, and vanilla until combined. Stir in the cream or evaporated milk. Slowly stir the egg mixture into the mashed beans, combining the filling well.

The filling can also be almost completely prepared in the food processor. In a processor fitted with the steel blade, partially mash the cooked beans. Add the eggs, sugar, molasses, cinnamon, nutmeg, salt, and vanilla and process until combined. Pour the mixture into a bowl and stir in the cream or evaporated skimmed milk.

4. Line a pie plate with the bottom crust and make a fluted edge (see page 128). Pour the filling into it and bake the pie for 15 minutes. Reduce the oven temperature to 350°F. and continue to bake the pie for 50 to 55 minutes, until the filling is nicely browned and slightly puffed in the center.

5. Let the pie cool on a wire rack before serving it slightly warm or at room temperature.

On Preparing Dried Beans

One cup of dried small white beans or navy beans yields about 2 1/2 cups drained cooked beans, which, in turn, will yield the 2 cups mashed beans needed for Bean Pie (opposite). Use only dried beans for this recipe—canned beans will not do! They are oversalted and overcooked.

To prepare dried beans, pick them over and remove any wizened beans or pieces of dirt or stones. Then rinse the beans and soak them according to the directions on the package. Use either the quick-soak method—allow slightly more than 1 hour—or the overnight method, when 6 to 8 hours will suffice for the soaking.

To cook, drain the beans thoroughly. In a saucepan, cover the beans with 6 cups fresh cold water. Do not add salt even if the label on the package says to. Bring the water to a boil, reduce the heat to low, cover partially, and simmer the beans for about 1 1/4 to 1 1/2 hours, or until tender. Drain, then let the beans cool. Refrigerate, covered, until needed.

Raisin Pie

One 9-inch double-crust pie

**Old-Fashioned Dough
(page 111) or Vegetable Oil
Dough (page 119)**

1 cup light brown sugar, firmly
   packed
3 tablespoons cornstarch
1 1/2 cups cold water
1/2 cup freshly squeezed orange
   juice
2 teaspoons grated orange peel
3 tablespoons freshly squeezed
   lemon juice
1 teaspoon grated lemon peel
2 cups dark seedless raisins,
   rinsed and patted dry with a
   kitchen towel (see Tip)
Heavy cream or egg glaze made
   by beating together well 1
   large egg and 3 tablespoons
   cold water

*A*ll of us spoke to our mothers often during the course of putting together this cookbook, and it was interesting to hear how frequently raisins were mentioned as a tried-and-true standby ingredient—one reason being that they are excellent keepers. Raisins were part of the pantry, and as such were stirred into cookies, into cakes, into muffins, even into pies. It is easy to understand their appeal. Sweet and a little chewy, they were a treat, especially during the bleak winter months when fresh fruit was hard to come by. They are even good for you! So with some valuable input from our Moms, we came up with a pie made with lots of raisins and some brown sugar, all of which is nicely balanced and also accented with the tangy flavors of lemon and orange, both the peel and the juice. This is a Saturday-night supper kind of pie, after the homemade macaroni and cheese with ham, the fresh steamed broccoli, and tomato salad.

1. In a nonaluminum 3-quart saucepan, combine the brown sugar and cornstarch. Stir in the cold water, orange juice and peel, and lemon juice and peel. Add the raisins. Cook over medium heat, stirring frequently, until the mixture thickens and comes to a boil. Continue cooking and stirring for 1 minute. Remove the pan from the heat and let cool to room temperature.

2. Preheat the oven to 425°F.

3. Line the pie plate with the bottom crust and pour the filling into it. Trim the bottom crust to a 1/2-inch overhang. Arrange the top crust over the filling; trim the edge to 1 inch (or 1/2 inch for the vegetable oil pastry). Fold the top crust under the edge of the bottom crust and flute the edges decoratively, pressing together with your thumb and forefinger. Brush the top crust with heavy cream if you have used the vegetable oil dough, or with egg glaze if

you have used the old-fashioned one. With the tip of a sharp knife, make several 1 1/2-inch slits as steam vents around the center of the top crust. (This is a juicy filling and if the vents are too small the pastry may split during baking.)

4. Bake the pie for 15 minutes, reduce the oven temperature to 350°F., and continue to bake the pie about 40 minutes, or until the pastry is golden brown and the juices are bubbling.

5. Let the pie cool completely on a wire rack before serving it.

Tip: The reason for rinsing raisins is an old-time one, to rid them of sand and grit that some raisins have even when packed. If you buy boxed raisins, meaning those from the supermarket and not from a health food store, this consideration can be omitted.

PIE DOUGHS

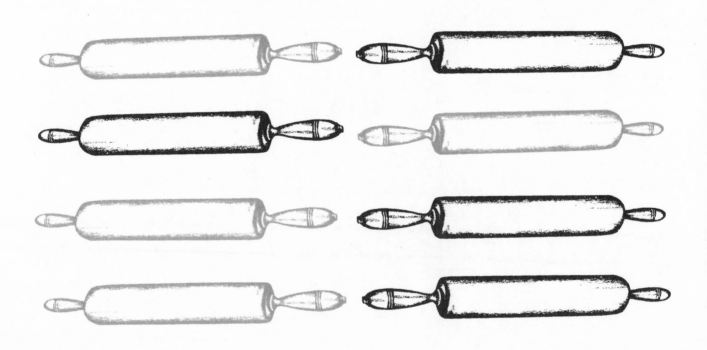

Helpful Pointers on Making Dough

Although dough making has scared off many a new baker, once you know how to do it, then sense your expertise growing, it is not only a wonderful accomplishment, but a pleasant and fun pastime, too. There is much to be said for simply doing it. Remember to be patient and to pay attention. Observe the stages as you do them. Practice, in this instance, really makes a sizable difference. The more you try it the more you will learn the feel of the flour on your hands, the amount of liquid to use, the direction to roll that little round of flour, shortening, and liquid so that it results in a round instead of a rectangle (!). It is not hard, but it does require repeated tries to get it down.

Whole books are devoted to the technique of dough and pastry making. Suffice it to say here that the pointers below are very important and will help you, as will the directions for the doughs that follow.

ABOUT MEASURING THE FLOUR: Bakers measure flour differently: Some scoop; others spoon. No matter what method of measuring you use, though, the amount of flour will always make a difference, particularly in pie doughs and pastries. Unlike other types of cooking, there can be no "a bit of this" or "touch of that" when making dough.

*We've worked with at least
seven pastries over the years.
We're down to about five now,
and we're very satisfied with
the ones we have. It's an
especially important point here
that the pastry complement the
filling of a pie and vice versa.
That's a process; it doesn't
happen overnight.*

—P.H.

BASIC EQUIPMENT

*Accurate measuring utensils—dry measuring cups,
    liquid measuring cups, and measuring spoons*
Wire whisk
Pastry blender
Large, smooth surface for rolling out dough
*Wax paper (for rolling Vegetable Oil Dough, in
    particular)*
*Plastic wrap and aluminum foil (for wrapping and
    refrigerating doughs)*
Rolling pin, preferably the ball-bearing type
Clear, flexible plastic ruler
*Sharp paring knife (for trimming dough, cutting lattice
    strips, and making steam vents)*
*9-inch pie pans—ovenproof glass—both standard and
    deep dish. (The standard 9-inch glass pie plate we
    use, measured from the outside from the bottom to
    the top of the rim, is 1 1/2 inches deep. The plate has
    a 4-cup liquid volume capacity. The deep-dish 9-inch
    plate is 1 3/4 inches deep and has a 5-cup liquid
    volume capacity.)*
Mercury oven thermometer
Wire rack (for cooling pies and prebaked shells)

As mentioned in the beginning of this book, the Little Pie Company bakers measure flour by weighing it on a balance scale. In preparing the recipes in this collection for home use, we measured the flour by the "stir and scoop" method. With a large spoon, stir the flour to lighten, actually aerate, it. Heap the spoon with flour and empty it into a dry measuring cup. When the cup is heaping full, level it with a single sweep of a straight-sided spatula.

ABOUT WORKING THE DOUGH: In general, handle the dough as little as possible and work quickly so that it doesn't warm and soften, requiring more flour during the rolling process. If the dough does warm and soften and there are problems with sticking, stop at that point. With as little handling or working as possible, transfer it to the refrigerator for no more than 15 minutes to give the fats a chance to firm up but not so hard that the dough can't be rolled, and then continue rolling the crust. Too much flour worked in as you roll makes the baked crust tough and dry. Know that excessive handling develops the gluten—the protein structure that forms the dough—and the more the gluten is developed by rolling and rerolling, the tougher the dough will be.

ABOUT ADDING LIQUID: Always hold back about 2 teaspoons of the liquid in a dough recipe. Variations in the amount of moisture in the flour or humidity in the air may make it unnecessary to use the full amount of liquid called for.

ABOUT STORING PIE DOUGH: To store dough in the refrigerator, wrap it tightly in plastic wrap or wax paper and aluminum foil. Store it no more than 2 days. (See below for returning it to room temperature for rolling.)

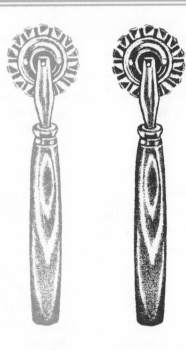

For longer keeping, know that pie dough freezes very successfully. To store it in the freezer, wrap the dough tightly in plastic wrap and aluminum foil. Label and date the package. Frozen dough should be used within 6 to 8 weeks. Let it thaw as directed below.

ABOUT PREPARING CHILLED DOUGH OR THAWING DOUGH FOR ROLLING: If the dough has been refrigerated overnight or for the maximum of 2 days, take it out of the refrigerator, but do not unwrap it, about 20 minutes before rolling it. Without that amount of time at room temperature, it will be too cold to roll easily.

Thaw frozen dough, wrapped, in the refrigerator overnight.

NICE TO HAVE ON HAND BUT NOT ESSENTIAL

Food processor
Bench scraper (for removing sticky pieces of dough from the rolling surface; made in both stainless steel and plastic)
Kitchen timer
Sugar shaker
Pastry wheel with fluted edges (for cutting lattice strips)

Old-Fashioned Dough

A generous amount of pastry for one 9-inch double-crust pie or two 9-inch pie shells

*T*his butter-and-lard–based dough is the one we choose for the company's fruit pies—the old-fashioned apple, peach, cranberry apple, blueberry, strawberry rhubarb. The butter and lard flavors are complementary to all of them, and especially to the apple pies. This is a flaky pastry, lightly sweetened, that rolls easily and handles well. We think the use of lard with the butter is the best combination for the flavor and consistency of the dough. However, use the vegetable shortening substitute if you prefer it, or if you have no access to high-quality lard with its fresh, pleasing smell.

This dough may be mixed successfully either by hand or food processor. To mix the dough by hand, we recommend that instead of using a pastry blender you cut in the butter and lard by rubbing it into the flour with your fingertips. That was the technique we used for many months before we were able to purchase our first professional 30-quart mixer and pastry knife attachment. The fingertip method keeps you in touch (literally) with the size of the pieces of butter and lard, and with practice your fingers will inform you of the optimal amount of "cutting in"—the moment when the flour and fat are ready for the addition of liquid.

The food processor technique we use calls for frozen pieces of butter and lard. Be aware that the capacity of the food processor bowl and the degree of hardness of the frozen fats are crucial variables in timing the amount of processing needed. We use an 8-cup capacity 450-watt food processor. If your machine is larger or smaller, processing times will vary. Frequently stopping to visually check the progress of the mixing will help prevent overprocessing.

This recipe makes a generous amount of dough, more than what is required for a standard double-crust 9-inch pie, but necessary for a high top, such as Old-Fashioned Apple Pie (page 17). Our philosophy is to be generous with dough. A larger amount is

2 1/2 cups unbleached
all-purpose flour

1 tablespoon sugar

1 teaspoon salt

8 tablespoons (1 stick) unsalted
butter, chilled and cut into
1-inch pieces for hand mixing
method, frozen and cut into
1-inch pieces for food
processor method

1/2 cup lard or vegetable
shortening, chilled and cut
into 1-inch pieces for hand
mixing method, frozen and
and cut into 1-inch pieces for
food processor method

1 large egg, beaten

1/4 cup very cold water
(refrigerated or chilled with
ice cubes that are removed
before measuring)

easier to roll. There is less chance of stretching and overworking the dough when rolling it out, and the excess is easily trimmed away. Extra pastry also lets the pie maker have greater latitude in determining the finished look of the pie. There is pastry for making decorative cutouts to place on the edges or the top. There will be ample overhang on both top and bottom crusts, necessary for making the sturdy, fluted edges that are recommended in several of the fruit pie recipes. High edges help keep the juices in the pie—where they belong!

Extra dough also makes possible the continuation of a generations-old tradition between pie baker and child. The scraps are perfect for practice sessions in dough rolling and handling. It is in these easygoing, impromptu times that the next generation of pie bakers gets its start. The dough may be reused and cut with a table or paring knife into free-form shapes, or cookie cutters may be used to do the job. Sometimes the irregular trimmings are simply placed on a cookie sheet to be baked. For special shapes and trimmings alike, sprinkle them with cinnamon sugar first and bake at 425°F. until lightly browned. Watch closely, as the time will vary according to the thickness and size of the pieces. Or, bake them plain and top with an all-fruit spread—raspberry or apricot, for examples. More advanced learners may want to use tiny tart shells for baking the dough, then fill them with their own special concoctions. Whatever the destiny for the extra dough, the goal here is to have fun learning.

The Hand Method

1. In a large bowl, stir together with a wire whisk the flour, sugar, and salt. Add the butter and lard. (If using vegetable shortening, see the variation on page 114.) Using your fingertips or a pastry blender, work the fat into the flour until the mixture forms pieces the size of peas. (It is all right if there are a few larger or smaller pieces.)

2. Combine the beaten egg and cold water. While stirring lightly with a fork, add the egg and water to the flour/fat mixture in a fast, steady stream. Continue stirring, occasionally cleaning off the dough that collects on the tines of the fork, until the flour is almost completely mixed in, but the dough does not form a ball.

3. Empty the dough onto a flat work surface. Work in the remaining flour by using the heel of your hand to press and push the dough just until it holds together. This is *not* kneading.

4. Shape the dough into a 6-inch disk. There should be many small pieces of butter and lard visible. Wrap the dough tightly in plastic wrap or wax paper and refrigerate it for at least 2 hours or overnight.

The Food Processor Method

1. Measure the flour into the food processor fitted with the steel blade. Add the sugar and salt. Pulse twice to combine.

2. Add the frozen pieces of butter and lard and process for 8 seconds, until the fat is the size of large peas. (If using vegetable shortening, see the variation on page 114.)

3. In a liquid measuring cup, combine the beaten egg and cold water. Turn on the machine and immediately add the egg and water, taking about 5 seconds to pour it in. Process an additional 5 seconds. Scrape down the sides and bottom of the bowl to help incorporate the flour more evenly. Process another 5 seconds. (Not all the flour will be incorporated.)

4. Empty the dough onto a flat work surface. Work in the remaining flour by using the heel of your hand to press and push the dough just until it holds together. This is *not* kneading. Shape the dough into a 6-inch disk. There should be many tiny flecks of butter and lard visible. Wrap the dough tightly in plastic wrap or wax paper and refrigerate for at least 2 hours or overnight.

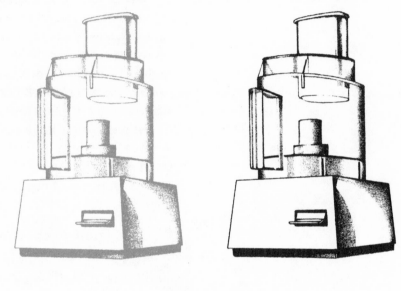

Variation

IF USING VEGETABLE SHORTENING

For both the hand and the food processor methods, if using vegetable shortening instead of lard, cut in or process the butter alone until it is the size of large peas. Then add the vegetable shortening and either it cut it in by hand or pulse several times to cut it into the flour. Proceed with the recipe as directed.

Light and Flaky Dough

*A generous amount of pastry for one 9-inch
double-crust pie or
two 9-inch pie shells*

2 1/3 cups unbleached
    all-purpose flour
1 1/4 teaspoons salt
3/4 cup plus 2 tablespoons
    vegetable shortening, chilled
6 to 7 tablespoons very cold
    water (refrigerated or chilled
    with ice cubes that are
    removed before measuring)

We use this dough for pies requiring a fully baked pie shell, such as Lemon Meringue Pie (page 78) and Banana Cream Coconut Pie (page 70). And because there is no sugar in the recipe, it is also our choice for Sugarless Apple Pie (page 32). The prebaked shells bake up light, flaky, and crisp and need no special attention—no pie weights, dried beans, rice, or foil to retain their shape during baking. The flavor here is subtle, not rich or sweet, making it a superb foil for delectable cream pie fillings. This dough is also a good choice for pies with fruit fillings, when a butter-based pastry is not desired. Last but not least, Light and Flaky Dough can be mixed up by hand, in a big bowl—the old-fashioned way.

1. In a large mixing bowl, stir together with a wire whisk the flour and salt. Add the vegetable shortening.

2. With your fingers or a pastry blender, cut in the shortening until it forms crumbs ranging in size from coarse meal to small peas.

3. Add the cold water either in a slow stream or a tablespoon at a time while stirring lightly with a fork. Stir until all the flour is incorporated and the dough clears the sides of the bowl and begins to form a ball. Shape the dough into a 6-inch disk and wrap it tightly in plastic wrap or wax paper. Refrigerate the dough for at least 30 minutes or overnight.

Rich and Tender Dough

One 9-inch double-crust pie or two 9-inch pie shells

2 cups unbleached all-purpose
    flour
1 teaspoon salt
2 teaspoons sugar
1/4 cup cold water
Half of 1 whole beaten egg
    (about 2 tablespoons)
1 1/2 teaspoons cider vinegar
3/4 cup plus 2 tablespoons
    vegetable shortening, chilled

*A*rnold's Mom sent this recipe to us during our first year of operation. We've used it ever since, making only a few small changes. It's a very tender and rich-tasting pastry, particularly good for such pies as Southern Pecan (page 91), One-of-a-Kind Walnut (page 99), and the three fresh pear pies on pages 26, 59, and 60.

1. In a large bowl, stir together with a wire whisk the flour, salt, and sugar.

2. In a small bowl or measuring cup, beat together with a wire whisk the water, beaten egg, and vinegar.

3. Using a pastry blender or your fingertips, cut the shortening into the flour until it is the size of small peas.

4. With a fork, stir the egg mixture into the combined flour and shortening mixture. Stir only until the liquid is incorporated and the dough begins to form a ball.

5. Dust your hands with flour and shape the ball into a round, flat 6-inch disk.

6. Wrap the disk tightly in plastic wrap or wax paper and refrigerate for 30 minutes or overnight.

Tip: Arnold's mother makes this dough in a double batch. (You have no leftover egg that way. You also have a ready-made reason for baking another super pie with it!) And the dough, when wrapped tightly, will keep in the refrigerator for 2 days. It may also be wrapped in plastic wrap and foil and frozen for 6 to 8 weeks.

Cheddar Dough

*Enough pastry for one
9-inch double-crust pie*

1 1/2 cups unbleached
  all-purpose flour
1/4 teaspoon salt
8 tablespoons (1 stick) unsalted
  butter, frozen solid and
  slightly thawed
2 tablespoons lard or vegetable
  shortening, frozen solid and
  slightly thawed
1 cup (3 1/2 ounces) grated,
  lightly packed New York State
  extra-sharp Cheddar cheese
1/3 cup very cold water

Cheddar dough was one of our first recipes, paired from the beginning with Granny Smith apples (see page 20), a winning combination that has stood the test of time. The dough is a special one, still made by us in small, two-pie batches. You will need a food processor; to make the dough by hand will not yield the unique texture and quality guaranteed by the quickness of the machine. One caveat about the processor, though. Be careful not to overprocess the dough. It combines in a matter of *seconds*, not minutes. This pastry would also be superb combined with Rhode Island Greening apples (page 38).

1. Put the flour and salt in the bowl of a food processor fitted with the steel blade.

2. Cut the cold butter and lard both into 1/2-inch pieces and add them to the processor. Process for 5 seconds, or until the butter is the size of peas.

3. Add the cheese to the processor and combine it with the flour mixture, using 2 on-off pulses.

4. With the machine running, pour the water down the feed tube in a fast, steady stream, adding all but 1 or 2 teaspoons, and continue to process until the dough just begins to form a ball, about 10 to 12 seconds.

5. Turn the dough out onto a work surface. If the pastry appears dry and crumbly, sprinkle the remaining cold water on it and work it in with your hand as you shape the dough into a 5-inch disk. If the dough is ready, work any remaining flour in with the heel of your hand, then shape the dough into a 5-inch disk. There should be many flecks of butter and cheese still visible.

6. Wrap the disk tightly in plastic wrap and chill it for at least 2 hours or overnight before using.

Working with Vegetable Oil Dough

Vegetable oil pastry handles most easily when it is rolled shortly after it is made. There is no need to let it rest or to chill it. If the dough must be held for a short time before rolling, wrap it in wax paper and let it stand at room temperature.

If the dough cracks or breaks during or after removal of the wax paper, simply press the edges back together. To repair a tear or hole, gently press a piece of scrap dough over the tear.

If you choose to use this dough for a latticetop pie, choose either the simple or semiwoven lattice design. All the folding and unfolding of strips required for making a woven lattice top will cause the strips to crack and break. Know that the fluted edge for Vegetable Oil Dough will be less thick and high, allowing the pie juices to overflow. Let Old-Fashioned Dough (page 111) work its wonders for you in this department.

When you need only one shell, either baked or unbaked, simply halve the recipe; it mixes up perfectly and very quickly.

Vegetable Oil Dough

*One 9-inch double-crust pie or
two 9-inch shells*

2 1/2 cups unbleached
　all-purpose flour
1 1/8 teaspoons salt
2 teaspoons sugar (optional)
1/2 cup plus 2 tablespoons
　vegetable oil, such as corn,
　canola, or safflower
1/4 cup plus 1 tablespoon cold
　whole or low-fat milk

*P*atricia's mother, who sent us this recipe, swears by this dough for ease in mixing and rolling, and so do we. It is perfect for custard and cream pies, with its flaky but crisp texture. Note that you roll the dough out between pieces of wax paper—now that does make it easy!

1. In a medium bowl, stir together with a wire whisk the flour, salt, and sugar if using.

2. In a small bowl, combine the vegetable oil and milk; it is not necessary to stir them together. Pour the milk mixture into the flour all at once and immediately begin to stir them together. Continue to stir until all the flour is incorporated. (The dough will appear crumbly.) Press the dough together, then divide it in half to form 2 round, flat disks. The dough is now ready to be rolled. There is no need to refrigerate it.

3. Cut four 12-inch squares of wax paper. Place 1 of the disks between 2 squares of wax paper. No flour is needed. Roll out the dough, using the edges of the paper as a guide, to form a 12-inch circle. Several times during the rolling process, flip the wax paper over so that the bottom becomes the top. Smooth out any wrinkles in the paper and continue to roll.

4. For a double-crust pie, peel off the top piece of wax paper. Lifting the wax paper up by the top corners, invert the dough into the pie plate. Remove the wax paper and ease the pastry into the pie plate. Trim the edges to a 1/2-inch overhang.

Repeat the rolling out of the second piece of dough, using 2 fresh sheets of wax paper. As before, remove the top sheet of paper, then position the top crust over the filling. Gently remove the remaining sheet of paper. Trim the edges to 1/2 inch. Fold the top edge under the bottom edge, flute the edges decoratively, and make steam vents. Follow the specific recipe for making steam vents, glazing, and baking instructions.

5. To prepare an unbaked 9-inch shell of Vegetable Oil Dough, divide the dough into 2 equal pieces and roll it out between sheets of wax paper as directed above for the double-crust pie. Ease the pastry into the pie plate and trim the edges to 1/2 inch. Fold the edges under and flute them decoratively.

6. To prepare a fully baked 9-inch shell of Vegetable Oil Pastry, roll, trim, and flute the edges as directed above for an unbaked shell. Next lightly prick the bottom and sides of the shell with a fork, making tiny holes that will close during baking.

Preheat the oven to 425°F. Bake the shell for 6 minutes. Remove from the oven and lightly prick the dough with a fork where it has puffed up during baking. Return the shell to the oven and bake 10 minutes, or until the shell is an even golden brown.

Pecan Coconut Crust

One 9-inch pie shell

2 cups packaged sweetened flaked coconut, chilled (see Tip)

1/4 cup finely chopped pecans

4 tablespoons (1/2 stick) unsalted butter, melted and cooled

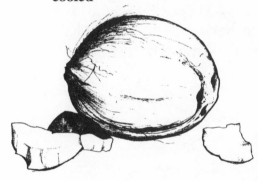

Here is a simple-to-make, press-in-the-pan-and-bake pie shell. Fill it with the chocolate cream filling on page 72, then top with whipped cream for a winning combination. Or try it with the banana cream coconut filling on page 70. For something simpler, just fill the shell with scoops of ice cream and freeze. Have an assortment of dessert sauces on hand for toppings.

When pressing this crust into the pie plate, be careful not to make the seam too thick where the side and bottom crusts meet. With a little extra pressing, you can achieve the desired 1/8-inch thickness. Professional bakers are "hard pressed" to do any better!

1. Preheat the oven to 325°F.

2. In a large mixing bowl, stir together the chilled coconut and chopped pecans. While stirring, pour in the melted butter and continue to stir until the coconut and pecans are evenly coated.

3. Empty the mixture into a 9-inch pie plate. With your fingers, first press the mixture evenly around the edges of the plate to a thickness of about 1/8 inch and up to, but not over, the edge of the rim, shaping a compact, level edge. (If the top edge is thin or has a lot of wispy bits of coconut sticking out, the flakes will burn before the rest of the shell has finished browning.) Press the remaining crust mixture evenly and firmly over the bottom of the pie plate. It will be about 1/8 inch thick.

4. Bake the shell for about 25 minutes, until the top edges are medium golden brown and the bottom is just beginning to brown.

5. Cool thoroughly on a wire rack before filling.

Tip: The reason for chilling the coconut is to firm the butter, which gives the crust mixture a more cooperative consistency.

Working with the Dough

I was taught that one crust should take one minute to roll out. That's basically correct. Ideally, it shouldn't take any longer than that. The bakers here can beat that time hands down.

—P.H.

The dough is made and now you're ready to roll!

How to Roll Pie Dough

1. Divide the dough into two equal pieces.

2. Shape each half into a smooth-edged 5-inch disk. If the kitchen is warm, wrap and return one of the disks to the refrigerator.

3. Place the disk on a lightly floured surface and sprinkle a small amount of flour over the top.

4. Roll the disk from the center out to the edges in both directions until it is about 8 inches long. Give the oblong piece of dough a quarter turn. Scrape away any pieces of pastry that have stuck to the rolling surface or rolling pin. Reflour the work surface lightly, using only enough flour to keep the dough from sticking.

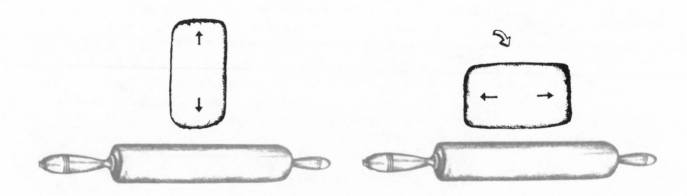

5. Continue to roll the dough out from the center until the shape begins to resemble a circle. Lift the dough and shift it slightly to make sure it is not sticking to the surface. If it is, scrape the surface clean and lightly reflour as necessary.

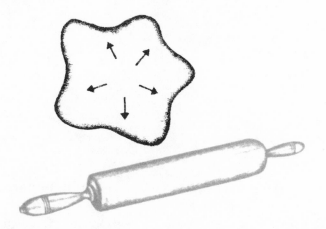

6. Before continuing to roll, it is important to press together any splits, tears, or rough spots around the edges of the dough so that the perimeter is fairly smooth. (Those small tears or splits will continue to grow during the rolling process and make the dough only more susceptible to tearing.)

7. To arrive at the size of the dough needed, roll the dough from the center out to the edges in all directions, being certain to lift the rolling pin up off the dough as it nears the edges. (This will help prevent the dough from being rolled too thinly at the edges.) As you are rolling the dough out to its final shape, occasionally run your fingers over the circle to feel for any too thick or too thin spots and gently roll those areas so the finished circle of dough is uniformly thick.

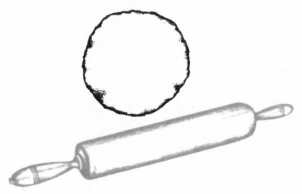

ABOUT REPAIRING TEARS IN PIE CRUSTS: To repair a tear, overlap the torn edges a tiny bit and gently press them together with a fingertip. If they refuse to mend, moisten your fingertip with water. Pat it over the torn edges and then press them together gently.

How to Prepare a 9-Inch Bottom Crust

1. Follow the directions for rolling dough, steps 1 through 7 on pages 122–23, into a 12-inch circle.

2. To transfer the dough to the pie plate, fold the dough in half; place the folded edge along the imaginary center line of the pie plate. Quickly and gently unfold the dough, then carefully lift the edges to let it drop, easing it into the pie plate and patting it into place without stretching it. Another easy way to transfer the dough to the pie plate is to loosely roll the dough up over the rolling pin. Position it over the pie plate and unroll it into the plate. Ease the dough into the pie plate, gently patting it into place without stretching it.

3. Fill the pastry-lined pie plate as directed in the recipe. Trim the dough edge to a 1/2-inch overhang unless otherwise specified in the recipe.

To Be a Baker

Making good dough takes practice and, like most other things requiring experience, doesn't come easily. Enjoy doing it; if you bring a lot of tension to making dough, the chances are you will have difficulties working with it.

The ingredients in pie dough are basic and few, but it is important to use the best ones you can. And always measure them accurately. Then comes the not-so-secret ingredient: technique, and that only comes with practice.

Even though you may have read a thousand times, don't attempt making pie dough on a hot day, it is still good advice. A hot kitchen, hot hands, and a hot temper from trying to pick up that sticky mass of flour and shortening are not conducive to the perfect round! On days when the temperature is soaring, serve the berries destined for Three-Berry Pie with heavy cream. Or, for an even more cooling choice, try simple ice cream.

How to Prepare a 9-Inch Plain Top Crust

1. Follow the directions for rolling dough, steps 1 through 7 on pages 122–23, into a 13-inch circle.

2. To transfer the dough to a filled pie plate, fold it in half. Place the folded edge along the imaginary center line of the filling and quickly and gently unfold it, covering the filling.

3. With a paring knife, trim the dough to a 1-inch overhang.

4. Fold the top edge over and under the bottom edge to make a smooth, even ridge of pastry all around the pie. If the edge doesn't look quite smooth and even when you've finished making it, use your fingers to gently press and shape the edge to redistribute the dough more evenly. The more even the plain edge, the more even will be the finished fluted edge. The ridge should be even with or slightly inside of the pie plate.

About the Juiciest

We designed the pie recipes in this book using pastry techniques to help keep the baking, bubbling juices within the pie, where they belong, and off the oven floor. Just the same, be alert near the end of the baking period—the last 15 minutes—to the sound and smell of juices cooking over. Only then, or if an overflow appears imminent, place a piece of aluminum foil, shiny side up, to catch any juices. While convenience suggests simply placing a piece of foil or a cookie sheet directly below the pie plate to catch the juices, both of those devices impede the circulation of heat in the oven and will prevent the pie from browning.

5. Use your fingers to flute the edges decoratively. (See How to Flute on page 128.)

6. Whether you choose the rounded or pointed style of flute, be sure the outer edges of the flute are within the rim of the pie plate. If they extend beyond, they may burn before the rest of the pie has finished baking. Or the edges may break off as the pie puffs up or expands as it bakes.

7. Brush the top crust with egg glaze or heavy cream and sprinkle with sugar as the recipe directs. Do not brush the fluted edges with either glaze or cream or sprinkle them with sugar. They will burn.

8. Make steam vents in the top crust as directed in the recipe—generally 5 or 6 vents, each 3/4 inch long, around the center top of the pie, but not near the edges because too much of the juice will escape through them.

9. Bake the pie in the middle of the oven unless otherwise directed.

How to Flute

Using the index finger and thumb of each hand, one hand positioned on the inside edge of the pastry, the other on the outside edge, pinch a small section of the ridge of dough between the finger and thumb of each hand. Release your fingers and move on to the adjacent section of dough. Again, pinch-release, then move on, continuing all the way around the pie. The finished look of the fluted edges will depend on the pinching technique employed.

For a wide, gently rounded flute: Keep the tension between your fingers and thumbs loose and relaxed as you pinch. This style of flute works especially well on those pies calling for a thick, high fluted edge, designed specifically to keep the juices inside the pie. Three-Berry Pie (page 51) is a good example.

For a sharply pointed fluted look: Keep the tension between your fingers and thumbs tight. Pinch the pastry on the outer edge until it forms a sharp but not thin (thin points will burn) pointed edge. This style of flute works very well on pies with a standard edge thickness and on pastry shells, such as the lemon meringue or chocolate cream pies.

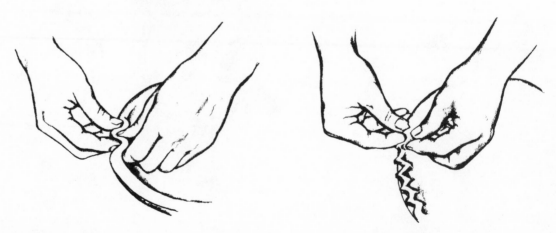

Latticetop Pies

How to Prepare a 9-Inch Latticetop Crust

1. Follow the directions for rolling dough, steps 1 through 7 on pages 122–23, into a 13-inch circle.

2. Have ready a ruler (the flexible clear plastic rulers found in sewing, craft, or art supply stores are perfect for this) and either a plain or fluted edge (fluted for the prettiest look) pastry wheel or pizza cutter, or a sharp paring knife. Measure and cut either twelve 1-inch-wide strips or eight 1 1/2-inch-wide strips.

3. Before separating the strips, brush them with egg glaze or heavy cream as the recipe directs and sprinkle them with sugar. (Glazing the strips at this juncture is very efficient and precludes any concern about glaze dripping into a pie filling. See Tip.)

4. Arrange the strips in a lattice design over the filling in a pastry-lined pie plate. (See the next section on the possible styles of strips.)

5. Trim the strips to a 1-inch overhang. Fold the bottom crust edge up over the edges of the lattice strips to make a smooth even ridge of pastry all around the pie. The ridge should be even with or slightly within the rim of the pie plate. Decoratively flute the edges.

6. Bake the pie in the middle of the oven, according to the recipe.

Tip: Glazing the strips before they are separated is very efficient, but try using less glaze, or omitting it altogether, within 1 1/2 inches of the ends of the strips. You will find it easier to make and flute the edge when the strips are not slippery with egg.

*Whether you are making a
double-crust pie or a latticetop,
you will need one recipe of the
recommended dough.
Surprisingly, lattice strips
use the same amount of pastry
as a plain top pie.*

How to Make Lattice Strips

Little Pie Company–style latticetop pies are made with 1 1/2-inch-wide strips placed on the pie to make a simple lattice top. We place 4 parallel strips across the filling and then put 4 more strips crosswise on top of them. We refer to this very easy-to-make lattice top as a "simple" lattice. It has the look of a lattice top without any weaving of strips. We like the look of big, wide strips on big, fat pies. There is, of course, more than one way to make a latticetop pie. You can vary the widths of the strips and use different methods of arranging the strips on the pie.

For a 9-inch-pie with wide lattice strips, roll the dough into a 13-inch circle and using a ruler as a guide, cut eight 1 1/2-inch-wide strips, for 4 lengthwise strips and 4 crosswise.

For a 9-inch pie with narrow strips, cut twelve 1-inch-wide strips, for 6 lengthwise strips and 6 crosswise.

After cutting the strips, choose one of the following three methods for arranging the strips over the pie in a lattice design.

Simple Lattice

Arrange 4 wide or 6 narrow strips over the filling. Place the remaining strips crosswise over them.

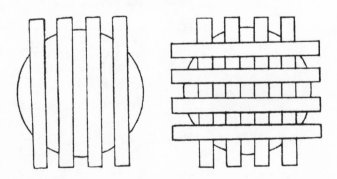

Semiwoven Lattice

Starting at one end of the pie, place a strip lengthwise over the filling. Place a second strip across it at a right angle. Continue to place 1 strip lengthwise, then 1 strip crosswise until all the strips are used.

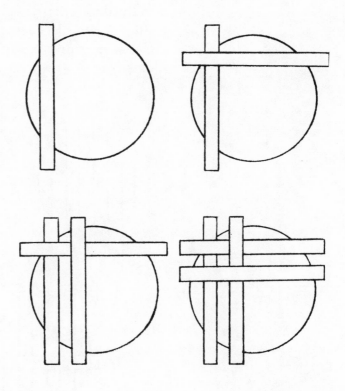

Woven Lattice

In this method, 4 wide or 6 narrow strips are placed over the filling parallel to each other. Then, working from the center out to the edge of the pie in either direction, crosswise strips are woven through them. The process involves folding back alternating vertical strips and placing a strip across the unfolded strips, as shown in the illustrations. Unfold the strips and fold back the alternate strips. Again, place a strip across the unfolded strips. When the last crosswise strip has been placed, repeat the process on the other half of the pie.

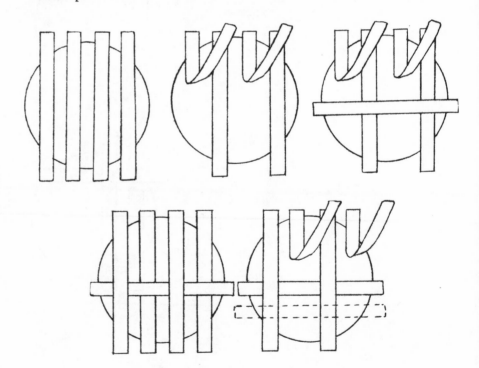

How to Prepare a Fully Baked 9-Inch Shell

1. Follow the directions for rolling dough, steps 1 through 7 on pages 122–23, into a 13-inch circle. If using Rich and Tender Dough, roll it into a 12-inch circle.

2. Fold the circle in half to transfer it to the pie plate. Place the folded edge along the center line of the pie plate. Quickly and gently unfold the dough, carefully lift the edges to ease it into the pie plate, and pat it into place without stretching the dough.

3. Trim the overhang to 1 inch.

4. Fold under the edge to make a smooth even ridge of pastry all around the shell. Decoratively flute the edges. (See How to Flute on page 128.) The fluted edge should be at or extend a tiny bit beyond the rim of the pie plate. This will help it to hold its shape during baking, preventing the edges from shrinking down.

5. With a fork, prick the sides and bottom of the shell.

6. Preheat the oven to 425°F.

7. Bake the shell for 7 minutes. Remove from the oven and with the fork prick any places that have puffed up during baking. Then with your fingers—be careful, for the dough is hot—or the back of a fork, push up and reposition any edges that are sinking. (If the dough was rolled and eased into the pie plate without stretching, it is not too likely that the sides of the shell will shrink down during baking.)

8. Return the shell to the oven for 12 minutes, until it is golden brown on the bottom and fluted edges. The sides will not be quite as dark.

9. Let the shell cool completely on a wire rack before filling it according to the recipe.

LITTLE PIES
of the
LITTLE PIE COMPANY

*L*ittle pies are absolutely adorable. They are like the smallest children in a play who unwittingly steal the scene from the lead. The audience cannot help but love them. Before your heart gets the better of you and you embark upon making a little pie, read the guidelines below; they will make everything about making little pies easier.

Dimensions

A little pie bakes in a 5-inch deep-dish recyclable aluminum tin and serves 1 or 2, depending upon your appetites. We found these tins, which look like little pot pie tins, in the grocery store. They actually measure 4 3/8 inches from rim to rim on the inside or 5 inches across the top, measuring from the outside of the rim. They are 1 3/16 inches deep.

Choice of Pastry

In general, choose a pastry recipe that handles easily; you will be rolling a lot of little pie crusts.

Old-Fashioned Dough made with lard (page 111) ranks best for handling.

Old-Fashioned Dough made with vegetable shortening (page 114) ranks second best.

135

Light and Flaky Dough (page 115) comes in third for handling.

Only more experienced bakers should attempt little pies with Rich and Tender Dough (page 116) or Vegetable Oil Dough (page 119), each for different reasons being tricky to handle in small amounts.

Yields

DOUGH: 1 dough recipe will yield 5 double-crust little pies, or 10 shells. (Ten shells is quite an undertaking at one time, however, and it is much more likely, and practical, for you to halve the dough recipe to make 5 shells.)

FILLING: 1 filling recipe will yield about 5 little pies. For the very best results, use cooked fruit fillings (they are the easiest to work with).

You will need about 3/4 cup of filling per little pie.

Fresh fruit fillings work very well, too. Simply divide the filling, as in Old-Fashioned Apple Pie (page 17), for example, equally among the 5 prepared little tins.

For the cooked cream pie fillings, fill each shell up to where the base of the flute starts on the rim.

Now that you know the variables, it's time to bake the little pies.

To Roll the Dough for a Double-Crust Little Pie

1. Divide the dough into 2 equal pieces.

2. With your hands, shape and roll each half into an evenly rounded 10-inch cylinder or log.

3. Cut each log into five 2-inch pieces. Use a ruler to measure.

4. Press each 2-inch piece into a 3-inch round disk.

5. One at a time, on a lightly floured surface, roll each disk into a 7 1/2-inch circle. This is the dimension for both top and bottom crusts (as well as for shells). The circle will extend 1 1/4 inches beyond the rim of an inverted little pie tin. Note that the dough will be rolled out more thinly than for a 9-inch pie crust. As each circle is rolled, ease it into a little tin without stretching it. Refrigerate the tin and continue onto the next one. Be sure to refrigerate each shell as it is finished.

6. Divide the filling of choice among the pastry-lined little tins.

7. One at a time, roll out a top crust circle and place it over the filling. Trim the top crust edge to a 3/4-inch overhang. Fold the top edge under the bottom edge and flute the edges decoratively. Make sure that the flutes are within the rim of the pie tin; otherwise they may burn or break off during baking.

8. Make 5 or 6 steam vents, each 1/2 inch long, around the center of the top of the pie. Glaze and bake the pie as directed in the recipe, with these important *exceptions:*

—Bake the pies on a dull cookie sheet.

—Bake the little pies according to the temperature(s) and time(s) given for the 9-inch pie, but be prepared to remove the little pie 5 to 10 minutes earlier.

To Prepare Fully Baked Little Pie Shells

1. Begin by making the pastry of choice, divide it in 2 equal pieces, and freeze 1 piece for use at another time.

2. Prepare the dough as described in steps 2 through 5 on page 137, fluting the edges and pricking the sides and bottom of each of the shells with a fork. Refrigerate for 1/2 hour.

3. Preheat the oven to 425°F.

4. Place the chilled shells on a baking sheet and bake for 6 minutes. Remove from the oven and with a fork prick any places that have puffed up during baking. Then with your fingers—be careful, for the dough is hot—or the back of a fork push up and reposition any edges that are sinking.

5. Return the shells to the oven for 10 to 12 minutes, until the shells have browned. The bottoms and fluted edges will be darker than the sides.

6. Let the shells cool completely on a wire rack before filling them with the desired cooked cream filling.

Tip: Know that fully baked little pie shells are a challenge to make successfully. The sides of the 5-inch tins are disproportionately deeper and steeper than those on a standard-size pie plate and because of this the shells have a greater tendency to shrink during baking. To help prevent the dough from shrinking unduly, make sure that the flutes are right at or a tiny bit over the edge of the rim. And remember not to overwork the dough.

CAKES

*T*here were some obvious, easy choices to be made when we first started to bake cakes at the Little Pie Company. Cheesecake, for instance. Everyone loves cheesecake. And carrot cake. And a moist apple cake, that was a must. And then, of course, a two-layer coconut cake, made with fresh shredded coconut—one of Arnold's favorites.

We also wanted a stand-out gingerbread, but it didn't come for a while. We experimented with all kinds of different variations to arrive at the one we have now, which is made with both fresh and ground ginger. It's spirited and tasty, lovely and dark in color—good for a nippy fall day. We're glad to have let it take its time.

Then there are the cakes that are slightly fancier: one that is marbled with chocolate and topped with a chocolate sour cream icing so easy to make you won't believe it. Angel food cake, snowy in color and tall, falls in this special category, and in the event you wanted to dress it up some, we've included a liqueur-flavored chocolate sauce. Only one of these showy cakes is multistep—the bittersweet chocolate torte—a recipe that came to us from a friend of Michael's. The cake is dense but tender, and we make it only for Passover. It has the decided advantage of being able to be made in

ESSENTIAL EQUIPMENT

One 9-inch tube pan with removable bottom
One 9-inch round metal cake pan, 2 inches deep
Two 8-inch round metal cake pans
One 8-inch square (2-quart) glass baking dish
One 13 by 9-inch metal baking pan
One 9 by 5 by 3-inch metal loaf baking pan
One 8-inch round, 3-inch deep metal cake pan or
   springform pan (for baking cheesecake)
Electric hand-held mixer
Food processor
Medium wire whisk
Wire cooling rack
Grater
Sifter
Double boiler
Icing spatula
1 1/2-inch pastry brush
Long serrated knife (for slicing angel food cake)

NICE TO HAVE ON HAND BUT NOT ESSENTIAL

Cake turntable or lazy Susan (for icing)
Pedestaled cake plate
Cake serving spatula

advance and frozen. Chocolate cakes, whether plain or fancy, are favorites, and there are some good ones here.

The cake that has won over our hearts, though, is the upside-down cake. Melted brown sugar, pineapple rings, and cherries atop a soft-crumbed cake take us back to those sunny days when we were sitting on the back porch and could hear through the screen door the timer go off, announcing that it would be only a short wait then to that sticky first bite. It was candy, it was cake, it was magic that it even came out of the pan. It's American baking at its most simple best.

Applesauce Carrot Cake

One 13 × 9-inch cake

2 cups sifted unbleached
    all-purpose flour
1 cup sugar
2 teaspoons baking soda
2 teaspoons ground cinnamon
1 cup Granny Smith Applesauce
    (page 30) or unsweetened
    applesauce, thick and smooth
1/2 cup egg whites (from about
    4 large eggs)
1/2 cup vegetable oil, such as
    corn or canola oil
2 teaspoons pure vanilla extract
1 1/2 cups finely shredded raw
    carrots
1/2 cup sweetened flaked
    coconut (the packaged
    variety)
1/2 cup dates or raisins,
    coarsely chopped
1/2 cup walnuts, coarsely
    chopped

*E*ncouraged by customer requests for low-fat, low-cholesterol products, we lightened up our original carrot cake, reducing the sugar and oil by half and eliminating whole eggs in favor of egg whites. Here is the recipe, which is lighter than a usual carrot cake but no less good. It is still loaded with carrots, walnuts, and cinnamon—all the things we remember loving in those homemade carrot cakes of our not-so-distant youths. Ours goes one step farther and has both coconut and dates, too. Take this easy-to-pack dessert on a picnic or serve it cut into squares on any happy family gathering.

This is also a great teaching recipe for children. They practice grating, chopping, sifting, and separating eggs. The batter is easy to stir together and the results practically guaranteed.

This cake keeps well for several days when tightly wrapped and stored in either a cool, dry place, or in the refrigerator. In fact, the cake improves in flavor as it stands. If you can wait that long, it tastes even better and seems to be more moist on the second or even on the third day.

1. Preheat the oven to 350°F. Grease and flour a 13 × 9-inch baking pan.

2. In a large bowl, stir together with a wire whisk the flour, sugar, baking soda, and cinnamon.

3. In a medium bowl, combine the applesauce, egg whites, vegetable oil, and vanilla.

4. Stir the applesauce mixture into the dry ingredients until well blended. Mix in the carrots, coconut, and dates or raisins.

5. Pour the batter into the prepared pan, smoothing it evenly. Sprinkle the walnuts over the top.

6. Bake for about 35 minutes, or until the cake tests done in the center—a touch with your fingertip should leave only a faint impression.

7. Let the cake cool thoroughly on a wire rack before serving.

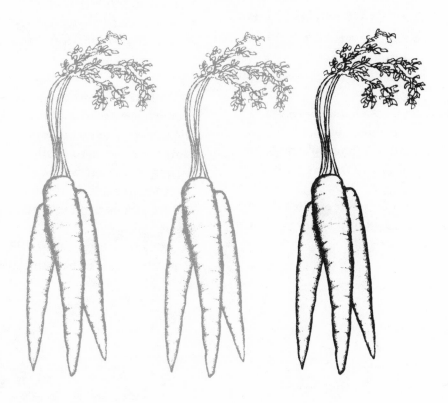

Pineapple Upside-Down Cake

One 9-inch round cake

THE UPSIDE-DOWN TOPPING

4 tablespoons (1/2 stick)
   unsalted butter
1 cup light brown sugar, firmly
   packed
2 tablespoons unsweetened
   pineapple juice
7 canned pineapple rings, well
   drained, reserve juices (see
   Tips)
12 glacéed or candied cherries,
   rinsed in very hot water and
   patted dry

*T*he memory of seeing Pineapple Upside-Down Cake for the very first time stays with one forever. It is so striking; the primary colors of light yellow pineapple rings and red cherries half-buried in sticky brown caramel, with yellow cake beneath! But too often the cake seems to get shortchanged. So we took extra care in developing the batter, making it light but not too airy, ensuring that it be the worthiest of companions to the tempting topping. Don't be surprised if a cherry disappears from the top sometime between the cooling and serving of this classic dessert.

1. Make the topping. In a small heavy-bottomed saucepan over low heat, melt the butter. Add the brown sugar and pineapple juice, stirring to combine. Increase the heat to medium-high and bring the mixture to a rolling boil. Lower the heat to medium and stirring frequently with a wooden spoon—not a rubber spatula—continue to cook for 1 minute. Handling it with care as the syrup will be very hot, remove the pan from the heat and let cool for about 5 minutes.

2. Pour the syrup into a 9-inch round metal cake pan 2 inches deep, and arrange the pineapple rings and cherries on it.

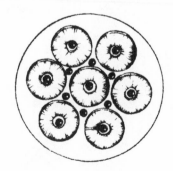

THE CAKE

1 1/2 cups sifted bleached all-purpose flour

2 1/4 teaspoons baking powder

Scant 1/4 teaspoon salt

6 tablespoons unsalted butter, softened

3/4 cup superfine sugar

2 large eggs, at room temperature

1 tablespoon unsweetened pineapple juice

1 1/2 teaspoons pure vanilla extract

1 teaspoon finely grated orange or lemon peel

3/4 cup milk, at room temperature

3. Preheat the oven to 350°F.

4. Make the cake. In a medium bowl, stir together with a wire whisk the flour, baking powder, and salt. Sift the ingredients into a bowl.

5. In a large bowl with an electric mixer on medium speed, cream the butter and sugar until light and fluffy. Beat in the eggs, one at a time, scraping down the bowl with a rubber spatula after each addition. Mix in the pineapple juice, vanilla, and peel.

6. Add the dry ingredients in 3 equal additions alternately with the milk, beginning and ending with the flour. After each addition scrape down the bowl and mix only until combined. Pour the batter evenly over the arranged fruit.

7. Bake the cake about 40 minutes, until a cake tester or wooden pick inserted in the cake (not the fruit) comes out clean.

8. Let the cake cool on a wire rack for 5 minutes. Then run a thin knife around the edges of the pan. Place a serving plate over the cake and invert the baking pan so that the fruit side is now the top. Serve slightly warm or at room temperature.

Tips: You will need one 20-ounce can pineapple rings packed in natural juice.

While testing this recipe, we found that the type of pan that provided the best results releasing the cake after baking was a heavy-gauge nonstick 9-inch round—no pineapple rings stuck to the bottom there!

Lemon Pound Cake

One 9 × 5 × 3-inch loaf cake

1 3/4 cups sifted unbleached
    all-purpose flour
1 teaspoon baking powder
3/4 teaspoon salt
1/2 pound (2 sticks) unsalted
    butter, softened
1 cup sugar
3 large eggs, at room
    temperature
2 teaspoons pure vanilla extract
1 tablespoon plus 2 teaspoons
    finely grated lemon peel
1/4 cup milk, at room
    temperature

THE GLAZE

1/3 cup confectioners' sugar
5 teaspoons freshly squeezed
    lemon juice
1 teaspoon unsalted butter,
    softened
Few grains of salt

*T*his pound cake is buttery and lightly lemony in flavor; the crumb is melt-in-the-mouth tender. Served in 1/2-inch slices, it goes well with either milk or tea, and is very good, too, topped with a scoop of sorbet or fresh raspberries. Sometimes our customers request it lightly toasted.

Lemon pound cake also makes a wonderful gift or hostess present. Wrap it in clear plastic film, then tie it, as we do, with lemon-colored satin ribbon.

1. Preheat the oven to 350°F. Grease and flour a 9 by 5 by 3-inch metal loaf pan (see Tip).

2. In a medium bowl, stir together with a wire whisk the flour, baking powder, and salt. Sift the dry ingredients into a bowl.

3. In a large mixing bowl with a hand-held electric mixer on medium speed, cream the butter and sugar until light and fluffy. Beat in the eggs, one at a time, scraping down the bowl with a rubber spatula after each addition. Beat in the vanilla and lemon peel.

4. Add half of the sifted dry ingredients to the creamed mixture and mix only until the flour is incorporated, scraping down the bowl as needed. Beat in all of the milk. Add the remaining dry ingredients, mixing only until the flour has been incorporated.

5. Pour the batter into the prepared pan and smooth the top evenly.

6. Bake the cake for 55 to 60 minutes, or until a cake tester or wooden pick inserted near the center comes out clean. The cake will have a golden brown crust on top and will have a split down the center.

7. Shortly before the cake is done, prepare the glaze. In a very small nonaluminum saucepan, combine all the ingredients for the

---

Overheard at the
Counter

WOMAN (with happy
five-year-old child): *"Oh, I just*
can't decide. What would you
like, Justin?"

CHILD: *"Everything."*

---

glaze. Stir the mixture over medium-low heat for about 1 minute, until the butter has melted and the glaze is hot—but do not let it come to a boil.

8. Remove the cake from the oven and place the pan on a wire rack. Let the cake cool in the pan for 10 minutes. Turn the cake out onto the rack, then brush the top with about half of the hot glaze. Brush the remaining glaze on the sides of the cake. Let the cake cool thoroughly. Store tightly wrapped in plastic wrap at room temperature for 3 days. For longer than that, refrigerate the cake.

Tip: If using a glass rather than a metal loaf pan, reduce the oven temperature by 25°F.

Fresh Apple Cake

One 13 × 9-inch cake

1/2 cup granulated sugar

1/2 cup light brown sugar, firmly packed

8 tablespoons (1 stick) unsalted butter, softened

2 large eggs, at room temperature

1 3/4 cups unbleached all-purpose flour

2 1/2 teaspoons baking powder

1 teaspoon ground cinnamon

1/2 teaspoon ground mace

1/4 teaspoon ground cloves

1/2 teaspoon salt

About 4 medium Golden Delicious apples, peeled, cored, and cut into 1/4-inch dice (you will need 4 cups diced apples)

1/2 cup finely chopped walnuts

Whipped cream, as accompaniment, if desired

A bakery that has had as much experience as we have turning out apple pies should have a good fresh apple cake, too, and we do. This one is simple and moist, chock full of apples, and lightly but fully spiced. It makes a perfect autumn dessert. It also begs to be made in advance, for the cake tastes even better on the second day. A good keeper, a piece of this would be a nice surprise in a school lunchbox or snack bag.

1. Preheat the oven to 350°F. Grease and flour a 13 × 9-inch cake pan.

2. In a large bowl with an electric mixer, cream the sugars with the butter until fluffy. Beat in the eggs, one at a time, beating well after each addition.

3. In a medium bowl, stir together with a wire whisk the flour, baking powder, cinnamon, mace, cloves, and salt.

4. Stir the dry ingredients into the creamed mixture. (The batter will be very thick.)

5. Add the diced apples and walnuts to the batter, stirring them in until evenly distributed.

6. Spread the batter evenly in the prepared pan. Bake the cake for 35 minutes, until the cake is lightly browned on the top and a cake tester inserted near the center comes out clean.

7. Let the cake cool thoroughly on a wire rack before serving in generous squares, topped with whipped cream, if desired.

Banana Bread

One 9 × 5 × 3-inch loaf

8 tablespoons (1 stick) unsalted
butter, softened
1 cup sugar
2 large eggs
1/3 cup buttermilk, at room
temperature
1 1/4 cups mashed, fully ripe
bananas (3 to 4 large) (see
Tip)
1 teaspoon pure vanilla extract
2 cups sifted bleached
all-purpose flour
1 teaspoon baking soda
3/4 teaspoon salt
3/4 cup chopped medium-fine
walnuts

This is not a heavy banana bread, but a tender, moist one, deserving of a light spread of sweet butter or softened cream cheese. We think it tastes and slices even better the second day. Toast it, too. You can also freeze loaves of this bread for another day.

1. Preheat the oven to 350°F. Grease and flour a 9 × 5 × 3-inch metal loaf pan (see Tip).

2. In a medium mixing bowl, cream the butter and sugar until light and fluffy. Beat in the eggs. Stir in the buttermilk, mashed bananas, and vanilla.

3. Into a medium bowl, sift together the sifted flour, baking soda, and salt. Add the dry ingredients to the banana mixture, stirring well until combined. Stir in the walnuts.

4. Pour the batter into the prepared pan and smooth the top evenly.

5. Bake the bread for about 1 hour, or until a wooden pick inserted near the center comes out clean. Cool in the pan for 10 minutes before removing to a rack to cool completely. Wrap tightly.

Tips: A pie plate is the perfect vehicle for mashing the bananas. Slice them into the pie plate, then use the back of a fork to mash them to a pulp.

If a glass loaf pan is used, be sure to reduce the oven temperature by 25°F.

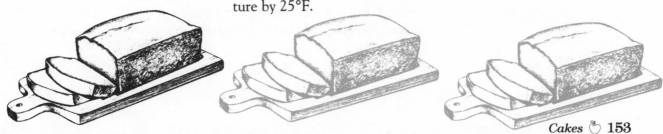

Fresh Ginger Gingerbread

One 8-inch square pan

1 1/2 cups sifted bleached
   all-purpose flour
2 teaspoons ground ginger
2 teaspoons ground cinnamon
3/4 teaspoon baking soda
8 tablespoons (1 stick) unsalted
   butter, softened
2/3 cup dark brown sugar,
   firmly packed
2 large eggs, at room
   temperature
1/2 cup dark sulfured molasses
2 tablespoons finely minced
   peeled fresh ginger
3/4 cup buttermilk, at room
   temperature

*O*ver the years many gingerbread recipes were tested before we arrived at this one. Some had sour cream; others light molasses. We think this is the best—moist, very dark (from both the dark molasses and dark brown sugar), and rich with the scent and taste of ground as well as fresh ginger. The cake is sweet, spicy, and tender, as we like to remember the ones our grandmothers made. It is superb as an accompaniment to Baked Apples (page 183) or served the traditional way, with applesauce. Eaten out of hand with or without a glass of milk, it passes all tests with flying colors.

1. Preheat the oven to 350°F. Lightly grease and flour an 8-inch square glass baking dish.

2. In a medium bowl, stir together with a wire whisk the flour, ground ginger, cinnamon, and baking soda. Sift the flour mixture into a bowl.

3. In a medium bowl with a hand-held electric mixer on medium speed, cream the butter and dark brown sugar until light and fluffy. Beat in the eggs, one at a time. Add the molasses and fresh ginger, mixing until combined.

4. Add the sifted dry ingredients in 3 additions alternately with the buttermilk, beginning and ending with the flour mixture. Scrape the bowl well after each addition and mix only until the ingredients are combined.

5. Pour the batter into the prepared pan and smooth the top with a spatula. Bake about 40 minutes. The gingerbread will be done when it has shrunk slightly from the edges of the pan and a wooden pick or cake tester inserted in the center comes out clean.

6. Let the gingerbread cool slightly on a wire rack, before serving slightly warm or at room temperature. Wrapped tightly in plastic wrap and stored in a cool dry place, the gingerbread will keep nicely for 2 or 3 days.

The More You Bake . . .

The more you bake the more you will be able to tell by the very appearance of a cake that it is done. The sides will be starting to pull away from the edges of the pan; the color will have that telltale tone of doneness. The touch will be right. Your confidence will soar. Almost equal to that, but not quite, you won't have to run around at the last minute looking for that elusive cake tester or toothpick!

Marble Cake with Chocolate Sour Cream Icing

One 8-inch 2-layer cake

2 cups sifted bleached
   all-purpose flour
3 teaspoons baking powder
1/4 teaspoon salt
8 tablespoons (1 stick) unsalted
   butter, softened
1 1/4 cups superfine sugar
1 large egg plus 2 egg yolks, at
   room temperature
1 1/2 teaspoons pure vanilla
   extract
1 cup milk, at room
   temperature
6 ounces (6 squares) semisweet
   chocolate, melted over
   hot—not boiling—water and
   cooled to lukewarm
Chocolate Sour Cream Icing
   (page 158)

This is a lovely cake to look at and taste, all frosted with swirls, then marbled inside with streaks of chocolate. It makes a superb birthday cake, and would cap an all-American dinner—the grilled steak, baked potatoes, and tossed salad variety—to a T. The icing is super, and a snap to prepare.

1. Preheat the oven to 350°F. Generously grease and flour two 8-inch cake pans.

2. In a medium bowl, stir together with a wire whisk the flour, baking powder, and salt. Sift the ingredients into a bowl.

3. In a large mixing bowl with an electric mixer on medium speed, cream the butter and sugar until light and fluffy. Beat in the egg and yolks, one at a time, scraping down the bowl with a rubber spatula after each addition. Beat in the vanilla.

4. Add the dry ingredients in 3 equal additions to the butter mixture alternately with the milk, beginning and ending with the dry ingredients. Scrape down the bowl after each addition and mix only until the ingredients are combined.

5. Stir 1 cup of the batter into the lukewarm chocolate.

6. Fill the pans with the batters, dividing them equally: First drop 5 or 6 large spoonfuls of white batter into each pan, using all the batter; then drop 5 or 6 small spoonfuls of chocolate batter into each pan, alternating it with the white and using all of it. To make the marble pattern, draw a table knife through the batter in each pan, weaving it through to create a marbled effect.

7. Bake the layers for 30 minutes, or until a cake tester or wooden pick inserted near the center comes out clean.

8. Let the cakes cool on a wire rack for 10 minutes before turning them out of the pans to cool completely.

9. To ice the cake, put one of the layers, bottom side up, on a serving plate. To keep the cake plate clean, tuck strips of wax paper just under the edge of the cake. With an icing spatula, spread on icing about 1/8-inch thick. Put the remaining cake layer, top side up, on the bottom layer. Ice the sides first, then the top of the cake with the remaining icing, making big swirls with the spatula. Remove the strips of wax paper before serving.

🍎 *Tip:* Icing a cake becomes a lot easier if you have a lazy Susan. Just place the cake on the serving plate and ice and turn until the cake is beautifully finished.

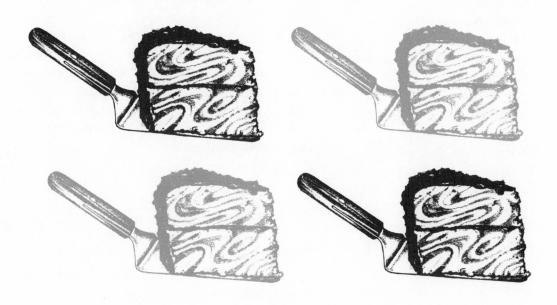

Chocolate Sour Cream Icing

2 3/4 cups

2 teaspoons instant coffee granules
1/2 cup sour cream
1 pound confectioners' sugar
1/2 cup plus 2 tablespoons unsweetened Dutch process cocoa powder
1/4 teaspoon salt
8 tablespoons (1 stick) unsalted butter, softened
1 teaspoon pure vanilla extract

*T*his recipe, a godsend for those of us who prefer not to fuss with making icings, came to us from our cookbook assistant, Dianne. She copied it down some years ago while watching a food-processor cooking show on television. It's incredibly quick and simple to make, without compromising on flavor or texture. The flavor is chocolaty, with the tang of sour cream and a whisper of coffee, and a texture so rich and creamy smooth that the icing glides over the cake. It may be mixed in either a food processor or with an electric mixer.

The Food Processor Method

1. In a small bowl, stir the instant coffee granules into the sour cream until dissolved.

2. Into the bowl of a food processor fitted with the steel blade, add all the ingredients, beginning with the confectioners' sugar and ending with the vanilla, followed by the combined coffee-sour cream mixture. Process for 15 seconds. Scrape the sides and bottom of the bowl with a rubber spatula, then process again for another 15 seconds, until the mixture is very smooth. The icing is ready for spreading.

The Electric Mixer Method

1. Dissolve the coffee granules in the sour cream.

2. In a large bowl, sift together the confectioners' sugar, cocoa, and salt.

3. To the sifted ingredients add the butter, vanilla, and combined coffee-sour cream mixture. Beat on low speed for about 1 minute, until all the ingredients are combined. Scrape down the bowl and continue to beat until the mixture is thoroughly combined and very smooth, about 15 seconds. The icing is ready for spreading.

Variation

For a really good mocha sour cream icing, use only 1/2 cup cocoa, and instead of the 2 teaspoons instant coffee granules use 2 tablespoons. Make the recipe as above, then use on your favorite butter cake.

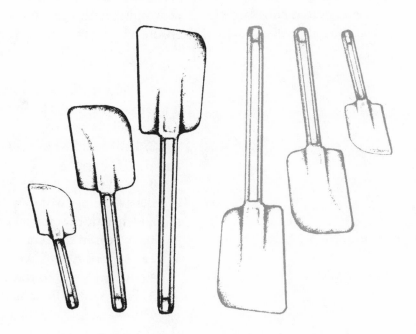

Angel Food Cake

One 9-inch tube cake

1 cup sifted cake flour (*not self-rising*)

1/2 cup plus 3/4 cup superfine sugar

1 1/4 cups egg whites (from 9 or 10 large eggs), at room temperature

1 1/2 teaspoons cream of tartar

1/4 teaspoon salt

1 teaspoon pure vanilla extract

1/2 teaspoon almond extract

*W*e make angel food cake when there is a surplus of egg whites from our Key lime pies. We often serve slices of it as is—a sensible, nonfat treat—but this cake's uncomplicated sweet flavor is adaptable to many dessert variations. Enjoy it with a fresh raspberry puree, for example; or top it with ice cream and drizzle it with a liqueur-enhanced warm chocolate sauce (page 162)—no longer a nonfat treat! For a more dramatic presentation, slice the cake horizontally into three layers, then reassemble it with fresh strawberries and whipped cream between the tiers. A super summer dessert, and an easy one.

To achieve a texture that is lighter than air—the reason, we suspect, for the name of this heavenly cake—we offer a few pointers at the end of the recipe for working with egg whites. They apply to working with egg whites, in general, and employed here will ensure a high-standing, celestial result.

1. Preheat the oven to 350°F. and put the oven rack in the lower third position. Have ready a 9-inch tube pan, preferably with a removable bottom.

2. In a medium bowl, stir together with a wire whisk the flour and the 1/2 cup sugar. Sift the mixture into a bowl.

3. In a large bowl with a hand-held electric mixer on medium speed, beat the egg whites until foamy. Add the cream of tartar and salt and beat until soft peaks form. Increase the speed to high and gradually beat in the remaining 3/4 cup sugar, about 1 tablespoon at a time. Continue to beat just until very stiff peaks form.

4. By hand, fold in the vanilla and almond extracts.

5. Sprinkle the flour mixture, about 1/4 cup at a time, over the egg whites and fold it in quickly yet gently. (The flour need not be thoroughly folded in until the last addition.)

6. Pour the batter into the tube pan, then pull a knife blade through the batter to break up any air pockets.

7. Place the pan in the lower third of the oven and bake about 45 minutes, or until the top springs back when touched lightly with your fingertip.

8. Invert the pan and let it hang upside down until thoroughly cool, about 1 1/2 hours. Actually put the center tube opening over a long narrow-necked bottle or use 2 same-sized cans as supports, placing them under the very edges of the pan.

9. To release the cake from the pan, insert a metal spatula or thin flexible knife along the sides of the pan. Pressing the knife flat against the pan, run it all the way around the sides and then around the center tube. Use a smooth motion. An up-and-down motion will leave zigzag tracks on the sides.

10. Invert the cake onto a serving plate and lift off the pan. If applicable, run a knife between the removable bottom and cake and lift it off.

11. Wrap the cake tightly in plastic wrap until serving time.

12. To serve, cut the cake into slices with a long, thin serrated knife, using a gentle sawing motion.

Tips: While the simplicity of an angel food cake recipe would suggest perfect results, take the following precautions when making it:

All mixing utensils and the tube pan must be grease-free. The least bit of grease may prevent the whites from inflating. And use a stainless steel bowl, not a plastic one, for beating the whites. Plastic bowls, even ones that have been washed squeaky clean, can harbor a fine layer of grease, which will impede the egg whites.

Separate the egg whites with care. A speck of yolk may prevent them from beating into peaks. If any yolk should fall into the bowl, use a piece of the egg shell as a scooper to get it out. The shell works marvelously, as anyone who has ever chased after yolk with a spoon knows!

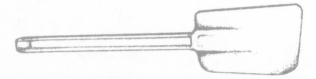

Chocolate Sauce

Makes about 1 1/4 cups

2/3 cup heavy cream
4 squares (4 ounces) semisweet
   chocolate, each square cut
   into 4 pieces
1/2 square (1/2 ounce)
   unsweetened chocolate, cut in
   half
2 tablespoons Amaretto

*I*f you serve angel food cake, low in fat in comparison to many other cakes, with this chocolate sauce, you will be undoing some of the good that you've gained. But we wager you'll be satisfying a craving . . .

1. In a small saucepan over medium heat, bring the heavy cream to a boil. Remove the pan from the heat.

2. Add both chocolates to the hot cream and with a rubber spatula stir until the pieces have melted and are blended into the cream. Stir in the Amaretto.

3. The sauce is now ready to serve. Pour it into a dainty serving bowl and place the bowl on a plate to catch any drips. Serve either slightly warm or at room temperature, with a pretty spoon or a small ladle.

4. Store any leftover sauce tightly covered in the refrigerator. To reheat, warm the firm, chilled sauce over hot water until it heats to serving consistency.

Bittersweet Chocolate Torte

One 9-inch round torte

Unsweetened cocoa powder for
dusting the cake pan
1/2 cup (4 ounces) firmly
packed pitted prunes
1/4 cup Armagnac
8 ounces best-quality
bittersweet or semisweet
chocolate, coarsely chopped
(set aside 2 ounces for use in
the glaze)
12 tablespoons (1 1/2 sticks)
unsalted butter, cut into
1-inch pieces (set aside 4
tablespoons—1/2 stick—for
use in the glaze)
3 tablespoons brewed coffee
1 1/8 cups shelled pecan pieces,
toasted (page 165), cooled
completely, and finely ground
in a food processor but not to
a paste
4 tablespoons cornstarch
3 large eggs, separated
1/2 cup sugar

$\mathcal{W}$e offer this torte once a year—at Passover. The recipe came to us from a friend of Michael's in Minneapolis, a caterer who made it initially, too, only for clients at Passover, but then on other occasions as well when a decadent flourless chocolate cake was called for.

This recipe is most efficiently prepared with two sets of bowls and beaters for the mixer—one for the yolks, the other for the whites. Failing that, try to have an extra pair of hands on hand to help with a quick wash-up of the bowls. By the way, the cake, unglazed, freezes well—something to be remembered should you be preparing it for a Passover seder.

1. Preheat the oven to 350°F. Grease a 9-inch round cake pan with vegetable shortening. Place a round of wax paper or parchment paper in the bottom of the pan and grease the paper. Dust the bottom and sides with unsweetened cocoa powder, knocking out any excess.

2. Several hours in advance of baking the cake or even the night before, soak the prunes in the Armagnac. Transfer the prunes and Armagnac to the bowl of a food processor fitted with the steel blade and process until the prunes are chopped into 1/4-inch pieces. They should not be pureed.

3. In the top of a double boiler set over hot—not boiling—water melt 6 ounces of the chocolate and 8 tablespoons butter together with the coffee, stirring frequently, until smooth. Remove the top from the double boiler and let the chocolate cool slightly.

4. In a large bowl, combine all the ground pecans, except 2 tablespoons, with the cornstarch.

5. Stir the chopped prunes into the chocolate mixture and add the mixture to the pecans and cornstarch, stirring until thoroughly combined.

6. With an electric mixer on medium speed, beat the egg yolks, gradually adding all the sugar except for 2 tablespoons (reserve it for use with the egg whites). Continue to beat on high speed until the yolks have greatly increased in volume and a ribbon forms when the beater is lifted.

7. In another bowl, beat the egg whites on medium speed until soft peaks form. Gradually beat in the remaining 2 tablespoons sugar and continue to beat until the whites are stiff but not dry.

8. Fold the beaten yolks into the pecan-chocolate mixture. When the yolks are fully incorporated, add the egg whites, folding them in quickly but gently with a rubber spatula.

9. Pour the batter into the prepared pan and bake 30 to 35 minutes, or until the edges test done. The cake will just begin to pull away from the sides of the pan and a light touch with your finger in the center of the cake will leave no imprint.

10. Cool the cake on a rack for about 1 hour. Then invert onto a cardboard cake round or flat plate. Wrap tightly in plastic wrap and chill, preferably overnight. The flavors will be better developed on the second day. Or freeze.

11. To finish the torte, about 20 minutes before applying the glaze, take the torte out of the refrigerator. (If the cake was frozen, let it thaw in the refrigerator.) Remove the cardboard round or plate and put the torte on a wire rack. Take care in transferring the cake; the torte is tender and somewhat fragile. Slip a piece of wax paper under the rack to catch drips.

12. In a small double boiler, melt the remaining 2 ounces chocolate with the 4 tablespoons butter over hot—but not boiling—water, stirring frequently, until melted. Cool slightly.

13. Using a pastry brush 1 1/2 inches wide, apply the glaze to the torte in 2 coats. Make the first coat a thin one. After it becomes firm or sets, apply the second, more generous, coat, using all the chocolate glaze. Before the second coat hardens, sprinkle the remaining pecans over the top of the torte. Refrigerate the torte for 1 hour to firm up.

14. With a wide spatula, transfer the torte to a serving plate.

15. To serve, slice into small portions. The torte is best served at room temperature.

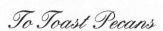

To Toast Pecans

Preheat oven to 375° F. Spread the pecan pieces in a single layer on a cookie sheet and toast in oven until the nuts begin to turn golden brown, about 7 minutes in all. Because they burn quickly, watch them carefully, stirring them around on the cookie sheet and checking them at least twice.

Coconut Cake

One 8-inch 2-layer cake

THE CAKE

2 cups sifted bleached
   all-purpose flour
3 teaspoons baking powder
1/4 teaspoon salt
8 tablespoons (1 stick) unsalted
   butter, softened
1 1/4 cups superfine sugar
1 large egg plus 2 egg yolks
   (reserve whites for icing)
1 1/2 teaspoons pure vanilla
   extract
1 tablespoon freshly squeezed
   lemon juice
1 cup milk, at room
   temperature

THE SEVEN-MINUTE ICING

2 egg whites (reserved)
1 1/2 cups superfine sugar
1/3 cup cold water
1 1/2 teaspoons light corn syrup
1 teaspoon pure vanilla extract
3/4 cup finely shredded fresh
   coconut (page 83)
3/4 cup coarsely shredded fresh
   coconut

*N*o question about it! A fresh coconut cake is a celebration in itself. Its peaks and swirls of coconuty icing make it irresistible. Do follow the tips for making the seven-minute icing and anticipate shredding the fresh coconut in advance. Coconut cake makes a wonderful birthday cake, high-standing as it is. Decorate it with fresh flowers for a very pretty presentation, and don't forget the candles.

1. Preheat the oven to 350°F. Grease and flour two 8-inch round cake pans.

2. Make the cake. In a medium bowl, stir together with a wire whisk the flour, baking powder, and salt. Sift the mixture into a bowl.

3. In a large bowl using an electric mixer on medium speed, cream the butter and sugar until light and fluffy. Beat in the eggs and egg yolks, one at a time, scaping down the sides of the bowl after each addition with a rubber spatula. Beat in the vanilla and lemon juice.

4. Add the dry ingredients, in 3 equal additions, to the batter mixture alternately with the milk, beginning and ending with the dry ingredients. Scrape down the bowl after each addition and mix only until the ingredients are combined.

5. Divide the batter equally between the pans. Bake the cakes about 30 minutes. The cakes will be very pale golden brown and will be just beginning to pull away from the sides of the pan.

6. Let the cakes cool in the pans on wire racks for 10 minutes, then invert the layers onto the racks to cool to room temperature.

7. Make the seven-minute icing (see Tips). In the top of a double boiler with a hand-held electric mixer on low speed, combine the egg whites, sugar, cold water, and corn syrup.

8. Place the pan over—not in—boiling water and beat on high speed for 7 minutes, until stiff peaks form.

9. Remove the pan from the heat and beat in the vanilla. Continue to beat for 2 to 3 minutes, until the icing reaches spreading consistency. Stir in the 3/4 cup finely shredded fresh coconut.

10. To ice the cake, place 1 cake layer, bottom side up, on the serving plate. To keep the cake plate clean, tuck strips of wax paper just under the edge of the cake. Spread the cake with icing, about 1/8-inch thick.

11. Place the top layer, top side facing up, on the iced bottom layer. Spread icing over the sides and top of the cake, making peaks and swirls in it with the spatula.

12. Sprinkle the remaining 3/4 cup coarsely shredded fresh coconut over the top and sides of the cake. Remove the wax paper strips before serving.

Tips: If you are making seven-minute icing for the first time, here are several pointers that will make it easier to complete. To begin with, don't try it on a humid day. Humidity will interfere with the whipping of the egg whites. Better to wait until a hot, dry summer day or a cold, dry winter day. Coconut cake in January; that's a dessert to lift anyone out of the winter blues.

Second, make sure the bowl and beaters are clean and grease-free, and that there is not a speck of yolk in the whites.

Third, the pan with the egg white mixture must be set over boiling water—not in it, and not over hot water—only boiling water will do.

Follow each of these pointers faithfully, and seven-minute icing will whip up to form lofty peaks.

New York Cheesecake

Makes one 8-inch cheesecake

2 pounds cream cheese, at room
    temperature
1 1/4 cups sugar
Pinch of salt
1 1/2 teaspoons freshly
    squeezed lemon juice
1 teaspoon pure vanilla extract
4 large eggs

If you have a food processor you have no excuse (save, perhaps, dietary ones) not to make this cheesecake whenever the mood strikes. Using the steel blade, it takes only minutes to blend a luxuriously smooth batter. Then it is just a matter of baking and cooling.

1. Butter the bottom, sides, and top edge of a cheesecake or springform pan, 8 inches round by 3 inches deep, and place a buttered round of wax or parchment paper in the bottom of the pan. If using the springform, line the outside of the pan with a piece of aluminum foil to prevent water from the water bath seeping in. Preheat the oven to 350°F.

2. Combine the cream cheese, sugar, and salt in the bowl of a food processor fitted with the steel blade. Process for 45 seconds, or until smooth. Add the lemon juice and vanilla and pulse several times.

3. Break the eggs into a measuring cup. With the machine running, add the eggs, one at a time, processing only until they are mixed in. Scrape the sides and bottom of the bowl and pulse several times to finish combining the ingredients.

4. Pour the batter into the prepared pan and smooth the top. Place the pan in a larger heatproof pan, such as a 13 by 9-inch baking pan or a roasting pan, and add hot water to a depth of 1 1/2 inches.

5. Bake the cake in the lower third of the oven for about 1 1/2 hours, or until the cake feels firm to the touch and has begun to brown. It will have risen in the pan but will settle as it cools. Remove the cheesecake from the oven and from the water bath and let it cool on a wire rack for several hours until it is room temperature. Cover with plastic wrap and refrigerate for at least 4 hours or overnight.

6. Remove the cheesecake from the pan. For a springform pan, run a thin knife around the sides of the pan and release and lift off the pan. For a 3-inch deep cake pan, run a thin knife around the sides of the pan. Then warm the pan over a low flame for about 20 to 30 seconds until the cake rotates freely in the pan. To finish unmolding the cake from either pan, place wax paper over the top and invert the cake onto a plate. Lift off either the bottom of the springform pan or the cake pan. Remove the buttered round of wax or parchment paper. Place a serving plate over the cake and carefully invert the cake right side up. Remove the wax paper.

Tips: At the Little Pie Company for Valentine's Day we like to bake cheesecake in a heart-shaped pan, then garnish it with a corsage of fresh raspberries glazed with apple jelly and a sprig of mint. Look for such specially shaped pans in cookware stores or even well-stocked hardware stores around the holiday.

Should your cheesecake crack on the top, it means that it is slightly overbaked; happily, the taste remains wonderful and unharmed. Just be sure to check the temperature of your oven before you next bake.

It goes without saying that you can make this cheesecake just as well with an electric mixer. With the mixer, beat the cream cheese until smooth. Beat in the sugar, salt, lemon juice, and vanilla, occasionally scraping down the sides of the bowl, until the batter is smooth. With the mixer on low speed, beat in the eggs, one at a time, scraping down the sides of the bowl. Combine only until the eggs are incorporated. Fill the pan and bake as directed above.

Cranberry Ginger Coffeecake

Makes one 8 × 8 × 2-inch cake

1 3/4 cups unbleached
  all-purpose flour
3/4 cup plus 2 tablespoons
  sugar
3 teaspoons baking powder
1/2 teaspoon ground ginger
1/2 teaspoon salt
8 tablespoons (1 stick) unsalted
  butter, melted and cooled
2 large eggs, lightly beaten, at
  room temperature
1/2 cup milk, at room
  temperature
1 teaspoon finely grated orange
  peel
1 cup cranberries, fresh or
  frozen, roughly chopped (if
  using frozen berries, see Tip
  on page 63 for chopping them
  and do so just minutes before
  adding them to the batter)

There is none of the usual coffeecake topping—streusel or glaze—on this coffeecake. Because of all the "noise inside," we have kept it "quiet" on top. With its tart red cranberry pieces, zippy translucent gold bits of crystallized ginger, and crunchy pecans, this tender, finely crumbed coffeecake is a brunch or breakfast treat that is very exciting to eat. Make it in the fall when the cranberry harvest comes in and the new crop of pecans has arrived on the grocery store shelves or is available through mail order. Serve it for a Thanksgiving or Christmas breakfast, and let one of the overnight guests—family or friend—help with all the chopping.

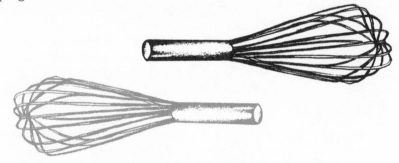

1. Preheat the oven to 350°F. Grease and flour an 8-inch square (2-quart) glass baking dish.

2. In a large bowl, stir together with a wire whisk the flour, sugar, baking powder, ground ginger, and salt.

3. In a small bowl, stir together the melted butter, beaten eggs, and milk.

4. Add the liquid ingredients to the dry ingredients at once and stir only until the dry ingredients are half mixed in. (Flour should still be visible.)

**1/4 cup crystallized ginger,
diced into 1/8-inch pieces
(see Tip)**
**1/2 cup pecans, coarsely
chopped**

5. Add the orange peel, cranberries, crystallized ginger, and pecans and fold them in with a rubber spatula. Fold only until the ingredients are evenly combined. Do not overmix.

6. Pour the batter into the prepared pan, smoothing the top.

7. Bake the coffeecake about 35 minutes, until the edges are light brown and the top is pale golden in color.

8. Let the cake cool in the pan on a wire rack about 45 minutes before serving slightly warm.

Tips: This coffeecake also bakes up wonderfully as muffins. It will make 12 standard-sized ones. Line the muffin tins with baking cups, divide the batter equally among the cups, and bake at 400°F. for 18 minutes.

Crystallized ginger can be tricky to chop. Some of it, also called candied ginger, comes in knobby, uneven pieces in glass jars sold in the spice departments of supermarkets. Another kind comes in boxes in perfect rounds usually sold in the baking section of supermarkets. Begin by slicing the rounds into 1/8-inch strips. Then stack the strips on top of one another and dice them into pieces. You want a small dice here; otherwise the impact of the ginger, sparky and delicious as it is, will be way too pronounced.

A Medley of American Favorites

*T*he Little Pie Company is only a stone's throw from the theater district on Manhattan's West Side. There are a lot of theater people who live nearby and stop in on a regular basis. We've baked many pies for company casts and opening night parties. It's always great fun. Theater people have their own kind of energy. It crackles almost.

It makes sense, then, given how near we are to Broadway, to call this last section of recipes a medley. It's a combination of our favorites, just like a medley of songs, and what all the desserts have in common is that we all like them a lot: They are American in heritage, and based on fruit—with one stunning exception, a peerless Brownie Pudding.

You will see once again our ongoing devotion to things baked with apples. We've baked them with crumbs, we've baked them with lattice strips on top, we've baked them in Cheddar dough, we've even baked them with some of their peel still on. Indeed, most of these combinations are simple, homey desserts, because it is hard to better a baked apple, whatever its final form.

We have Patricia to thank for Orange Caramel Cup Custards, those pleasing small cups of our past, and the recipe for Rhubarb

Pie-Crunch that belongs to her family. This crunch, unlike the dessert called a crisp, has a really crisp topping and a fantastic pastry beneath. Its sweetened rhubarb filling will make you long for spring.

The two cobblers in this group can be traced right back to Arnold's grandmother. He watched her make them as a child in California. He knew how she did it: She used lush California peaches. But we didn't dare want to use an imperfect peach, so we used dried ones, which turn out very good, too.

What's nice about a medley of favorites is that each dessert is different and not easily forgettable, making a reprise a sure thing.

BASIC EQUIPMENT

One 8-inch square (2-quart) glass baking dish
Six custard cups (6 ounces each)
One 13 by 9-inch metal baking pan (for water bath)
One 1-quart glass baking dish
One 2-quart round glass casserole
One large skillet
Clear plastic ruler and a sharp knife (or a pastry
*   wheel, for cutting lattice strips)*

Apple Brown Betty

Makes one 8-inch square dessert
6 generous servings

1 tablespoon unsalted butter for
  greasing the baking dish
1/4 cup golden or dark raisins
3/4 cup apple cider
2/3 cup firmly packed dark
  brown sugar
1 teaspoon ground cinnamon
1/2 teaspoon ground mace
1/4 teaspoon salt
5 large Granny Smith apples,
  about 2 1/4 pounds,
  quartered, peeled, and cored
  (cut each quarter into 3
  wedges to make roughly 6
  cups)
1 tablespoon freshly squeezed
  lemon juice
1 teaspoon grated lemon zest
8 tablespoons (1 stick) unsalted
  butter, melted
About 6 slices white sandwich
  bread, torn by hand to make 4
  cups coarse, 1/2- to 3/4-inch
  irregular fresh bread crumbs
Ice cream or heavy cream

A betty—a dessert made of layers of fruit, buttered bread crumbs, and spices—can have as few as four ingredients or as many as we have included below. No matter the number, the net effect of this dessert, as people discovered long ago, is the same. It comforts. It's sweet, soothing, and warm, and for good reason both children and grown-ups like it. And it's easy to make.

1. Preheat the oven to 375°F. Grease the sides and bottom of an 8-inch square (2-quart) glass baking dish with the tablespoon of butter.

2. In a small saucepan, bring the raisins and cider to a boil and simmer for 5 minutes. Let cool.

3. In a small bowl, stir together with a wire whisk the brown sugar, cinnamon, mace, and salt.

4. In a large bowl, toss together the apple slices, lemon juice, and zest. Stir in the cooled raisins and cider.

5. In a bowl, drizzle the butter over the bread crumbs, tossing the mixture together with a spoon.

6. Assemble the betty in the following order: Scatter one-quarter of the buttered crumbs over the bottom of the baking dish, top with half the apple mixture, sprinkle with half the sugar mixture, top with one-third of the crumbs. Spoon the remaining apple mixture over the crumbs; reserve 2 tablespoons of the sugar mixture, then sprinkle the remaining sugar mixture over the apples; top with the remaining crumbs, and sprinkle them with the reserved cinnamon sugar.

7. Bake the dessert for 50 to 55 minutes, until the apples are tender and the crumbs are browned.

8. Let the betty cool for 30 minutes before serving it slightly warm with ice cream or heavy cream, if desired.

Cheddar Crust Pocket Pies with Apples

Eight 6-inch triangular pocket pies

Cheddar Dough (page 117), chilled

3 large baking apples, such as Golden Delicious, Granny Smith, or Rhode Island Greening, about 1 1/2 pounds
2 tablespoons unsalted butter
1/4 cup sugar, plus additional for sprinkling on the tops of the pies
1/2 teaspoon ground cinnamon
1 tablespoon freshly squeezed lemon juice
Egg glaze made by beating together well 1 large egg and 3 tablespoons cold water

*P*ocket pies are the epitome of eat-on-the-run desserts. They fit right into your hand and, unlike ice cream cones or bars, they don't have to be eaten quickly before they melt. Like turnovers, lots of these have probably found their way into lunchboxes and picnic baskets alike. You could even eat one of them out of hand on the way to school or the office.

We've chosen our most sophisticated pastry for this informal type of pie. The dough bakes up so crisp and flaky it virtually shatters when you bite into it—so watch out for those crumbs!

These pocket pies are at their flaky best when eaten the same day they are baked. Wrapped and stored in the refrigerator, the pastry looses its crispness and its splendid ability to shatter. Rewarming in a preheated 350°F. oven for 10 minutes restores only some of the original crispness.

1. Quarter, core, and peel the apples. Cut the quarters crosswise into 1/8-inch slices.

2. In a large skillet or sauté pan over medium heat, melt the butter. Add the apple slices and cook them, stirring often, for 7 or 8 minutes, until they are almost tender.

3. Spoon the apples into a bowl. Add the sugar, cinnamon, and lemon juice and toss gently to combine. Cover and refrigerate the apple filling for about 1 hour, until completely cooled.

4. Drain the chilled filling into a colander set over a bowl and reserve the juices. You should have about 2 cups sliced apples.

5. Preheat the oven to 400°F.

6. Divide the Cheddar dough in half and shape each half into a square. Working with one half at a time, on a lightly floured surface, roll the dough out into a 10-inch square. Use a ruler and a sharp knife to trim away the uneven edges.

It may be hard to believe after making all the pies I have, but I still like to eat pie. Oh yes, I like pie.

—*P.H.*

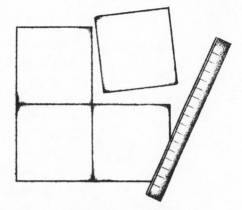

7. Using the ruler as a guide, cut the dough into quarters.

8. Assemble the pocket pies one at a time. Place a scant 1/4 cup of the drained apple filling in the lower half of each dough square and spread the filling out along the fold line and to within 1/2 inch of the edges. Spoon 1 teaspoon of the reserved juices over the filling.

9. With a pastry brush, paint a 1/2-inch-wide strip of egg glaze around all the edges of the dough.

10. Fold the dough over the filling on the diagonal until the edges of the dough meet. Use the tines of a fork to press and seal the edges together, making a 1/2-inch border. Make steam vents by piercing the top of the dough with the fork 3 times.

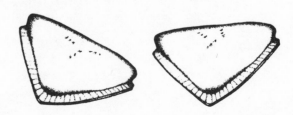

11. Use a large metal spatula to transfer the pocket pie to a baking sheet, placing it with the pointed side facing toward the middle of the sheet and being careful not to stretch the pointed edges.

12. Continue to make pocket pies with the remaining Cheddar dough squares and filling. Place a total of 4 pies on a baking sheet, with the pointed sides facing in toward the middle. Roll out the remaining piece of dough and make pies with the remaining filling, transferring them as they are done to a baking sheet.

13. Bake the pocket pies for about 30 minutes. Ten minutes before the end of the baking time, brush the pies with the egg glaze and sprinkle the tops with sugar. The pies are done when the pastry is medium golden brown in color.

14. Use a large metal spatula to transfer the pies immediately to a wire rack to cool before serving them either slightly warm or at room temperature.

Baked Apples

6 small baked apples

1 1/2 cups apple cider
4 tablespoons (1/2 stick)
  unsalted butter, cut into
  1/2-inch pieces
1/2 cup pure maple syrup
1/2 teaspoon ground cinnamon
6 small baking apples, about 5
  ounces each or 2 pounds in
  all, such as Golden Delicious,
  Ida Red, Cortland, or Macoun
1/3 cup assorted dried fruits,
  such as a combination of
  dried apricots, pitted prunes,
  dates, figs, or raisins, cut into
  1/4-inch dice

*W*hen we first offered baked apples at the Little Pie Company, they were stuffed with a rich, heady mincemeat and wrapped in pastry. Now, eight years later, we prefer them filled with an assortment of dried fruits—whatever we have on hand (we're partial to dried apricots)—and baked in an apple and maple-flavored syrup. Select small apples; they bake up prettily and finishing one completely comes with no effort at all. You might even want to serve these for breakfast. A baked apple a day . . .

1. Preheat the oven to 375°F.

2. In a small saucepan, bring the cider to a boil over moderately high heat and continue to boil it for about 10 minutes, or until it has been reduced by half. Remove from the heat.

3. Add the butter to the cider, stirring occasionally, until melted. Whisk in the maple syrup and cinnamon until blended.

4. Carefully wash the apples. Remove a 1 1/2-inch strip of peel from around the top of each apple. Core the apples to within 1/4 inch of the blossom end. Gently stuff the apples with the mixed dried fruits. Place the apples in a 9-inch square or round glass baking dish.

5. Pour the hot syrup over and around the apples.

6. Bake the apples for 40 to 50 minutes, basting them several times. The apples are done when they can be easily pierced with a paring knife.

7. Let the apples cool slightly on a wire rack before serving them warm in small bowls with the syrup poured over the top.

Apple Crumb Dessert

One 8-inch square dessert

1 teaspoon unsalted butter,
  softened, for buttering the
  dish

THE FILLING

6 apples, about 2 1/2 pounds,
  such as Ida Red, Macoun, or
  other baking apples that are
  not too sweet
2 teaspoons freshly squeezed
  lemon juice
2 tablespoons sugar
1 1/2 tablespoons cornstarch
1/4 teaspoon ground cinnamon

THE CRUMB TOPPING

1/2 cup unbleached all-purpose
  flour
1/4 cup granulated sugar
1/4 cup dark brown sugar,
  firmly packed
1/2 teaspoon grated lemon zest
1/4 teaspoon ground cinnamon
1/4 teaspoon ground ginger

*T*his is another apple dessert that is perfect for a family brunch or any other time when a quick-to-prepare, slow-to-bake, homey finale is called for. The topping is truly crunchy and crisp, with soft cooked fruit beneath. We've left the peels on the apples. When we were first tasting this, we had used half peeled half unpeeled ones, but found that we liked the color and texture of the peel so well— Was it that it reminded us of baked apples?—we decided to use unpeeled apples exclusively. You can imagine a dessert like this being served at a large wood table on a farm, the last rays of the setting sun shining through the windows.

1. Preheat the oven to 350°F. Butter an 8-inch square (2-quart) glass baking dish with the teaspoon of butter.

2. Prepare the filling. Wash the apples carefully and pat them dry. Cut each apple into quarters and with a small paring knife remove the core from each wedge. Slice each quarter into 3 pieces.

3. In a large bowl, toss the apple slices with the lemon juice.

4. In a small bowl, stir together the sugar, cornstarch, and cinnamon.

5. Add the sugar mixture to the apples and toss until the slices are evenly coated.

6. Prepare the topping. In a food processor fitted with the steel blade, combine the flour, both sugars, lemon zest, spices, and salt. Add the butter and process until the mixture forms fine crumbs.

To prepare by hand, in a medium bowl, combine well all the dry ingredients and the lemon zest. Use your fingertips to cut in the butter until the dry ingredients are incorporated and the topping forms fine crumbs.

1/4 teaspoon ground mace

1/8 teaspoon salt

4 tablespoons (1/2 stick) cold unsalted butter, cut into 1/2-inch pieces

7. Spoon the apples and any juice that has accumulated into the prepared baking dish. With your hands, gently press the apples down to make as level a surface as possible.

8. Sprinkle the crumb topping over the apples.

9. Bake the dessert for about 1 hour, until the juices are bubbling and the crumb topping is lightly browned.

10. Let the dessert cool on a wire rack. (The apples will settle as they cool.) Serve slightly warm or chilled. This dessert is juicy when still warm, so spoon it into bowls or saucers.

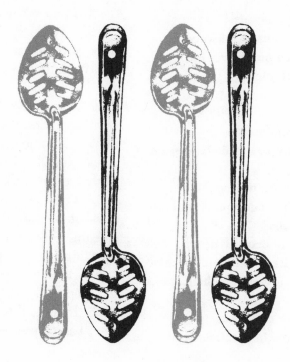

Rhubarb Pie-Crunch

One 8-inch square dessert

THE BOTTOM CRUST

1/2 cup unbleached all-purpose
   flour
1/3 cup light brown sugar,
   firmly packed
1/4 teaspoon salt
8 tablespoons (1 stick) cold
   unsalted butter, cut into
   1/2-inch pieces

THE RHUBARB TOPPING

1 cup granulated sugar
1/2 cup unbleached all-purpose
   flour
3/4 teaspoon baking powder
1/4 teaspoon ground cardamom
2 large eggs
2 1/2 cups diced (1/2-inch) pink
   or red fresh rhubarb, three or
   four 3/4- to 1-inch-thick stalks

Vanilla ice cream, as
   accompaniment, if desired

This rhubarb recipe from Patricia's family recipe file gave us pause when we tried to categorize it. Should it be placed among the pies or among the desserts? By virtue of the topping it qualifies as a crunch, since the batter bakes into a sugary, glazed, crunchy top crust. But underneath it has a greater resemblance to a pie; there is a custardy rhubarb filling and a bottom crust, buttery and toffee flavored. Hence Rhubarb Pie-Crunch—an especially good and homey dessert!

1. Preheat the oven to 350°F.

2. Prepare the bottom crust. In the bowl of a food processor fitted with the steel blade, combine the flour, brown sugar, and salt. With the machine off, add the cold butter, then process until the dough begins to form a ball. There should still be many tiny flecks of butter visible.

To prepare the dough by hand, combine the dry ingredients in a bowl. Use your fingers or a spoon to work the butter into the flour mixture until it forms a soft dough. (The butter need not be perfectly blended in.)

3. Press the dough evenly into an 8-inch square ungreased glass baking dish. (This can be a sticky dough. If you have difficulty pressing it into the pan, try placing a square of wax paper under your fingers as you press it into place.)

4. Bake the crust for 15 minutes. Let cool on a wire rack while you prepare the topping.

5. In a small bowl, stir together with a wire whisk the sugar, flour, baking powder, and cardamom.

6. In a bowl, beat the eggs until light and foamy. Whisk the dry ingredients into the eggs, then stir in the rhubarb. Pour the topping over the crust.

7. Bake the dessert for 40 to 45 minutes, until the top is lightly browned and crisply crusted.

8. Let the crunch cool slightly on a wire rack before serving it warm, with just a dollop of vanilla ice cream, if desired.

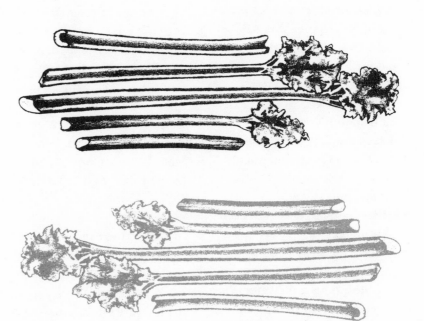

Apple Cobbler

One 2-quart round casserole

1/2 recipe Old-Fashioned Dough (page 111)

3 pounds (about 9) Empire apples, or other sweet (*not* tart), juicy apples that will hold their shape during baking
1/2 cup light brown sugar, firmly packed
2 tablespoons cornstarch
3/4 teaspoon ground cinnamon
1/8 teaspoon grated nutmeg
3 tablespoons unsalted butter
1/4 cup apple cider
2 tablespoons freshly squeezed lemon juice
Egg glaze made by beating together well 1 large egg and 3 tablespoons cold water
Granulated sugar for sprinkling on the lattice strips
Vanilla ice cream, as accompaniment, if desired

*H*ere is a cobbler made "Arnold's way." For most people, cobbler implies a "cobbled" or casually spooned-on biscuit topping, or a biscuit topping that is "cobbled up," put together roughly. Arnold's cobblers, which came to him from his mother (who learned how to make them by watching *her* mother), are juicy, cooked fruit mixtures topped with a lattice pastry crust, then baked. In fact, many cobbler recipes in Southern cookbooks do use pastry, but they call for two layers—one usually in the middle of the filling and the other over the top. We have had many cobbler topping "discussions" over the years and Arnold's way always prevails. When you're the owner, certain eccentricities are allowed!

As to the type of apple, we tried many and after a lot of tastings found we liked Empire apples best. They are sweet and cook up juicy and tender. It is coincidental—but what coincidence!—we would opt for Empire apples—they are named after New York State. Although they are probably not served for breakfast, cobblers like this one should be. Again, we have Arnold's grandmother and mother to thank for this recipe.

1. Preheat the oven to 425°F.

2. Quarter, core, and peel the apples. Cut each quarter into 2 wedges. They will make roughly 7 cups.

3. In a small bowl, stir together with a wire whisk the brown sugar, cornstarch, cinnamon, and nutmeg.

4. In a large skillet over medium heat, melt the butter. Add the apples and stir in the sugar mixture, cider, and lemon juice. Continue to cook the apples for about 10 minutes, stirring frequently, to prevent the thickening juices from scorching. (The slices will still be firm at the end of the cooking time.)

It's like watching a flower bloom. That's the stage we're at at the Little Pie Company. We need to continue to be careful, to let it evolve, and grow.

—M.D.

5. Transfer the apples and all their juices to a 2-quart casserole. Let stand while you roll out the lattice strips.

6. On a lightly floured surface, roll the dough into a 13-inch round and cut out eight 1 1/2-inch-wide strips. Before separating the strips, brush them with the egg glaze and sprinkle them with granulated sugar. Arrange the strips in a lattice design over the warm apples. (If you are making a woven-type lattice top, work quickly because the warm apples will soften the dough strips and they will stretch during the weaving process.) Trim the lattice strips even with the top edge of the baking dish. They will shrink down to the level of the filling during baking.

7. Bake the cobbler for 35 minutes, or until the pastry is dark golden brown and the juices are bubbling.

8. Let the cobbler cool slightly on a wire rack before serving—with vanilla ice cream, if desired.

Dried Peach Cobbler

One 2-quart round casserole

1/2 recipe Old-Fashioned
    Dough (page 111)

12 ounces sulfured dried peach
    halves, about 15 halves, each
    cut into 4 strips
2 1/2 cups water
1 cup apple cider
3 tablespoons instant tapioca
1/3 cup granulated sugar, plus
    additional for sprinkling on
    top
1/3 cup light brown sugar,
    firmly packed
1/4 teaspoon grated nutmeg
2 tablespoons freshly squeezed
    lemon juice
3 tablespoons unsalted butter
Egg glaze made by beating
    together well 1 large egg and
    3 tablespoons cold water
Vanilla ice cream, as
    accompaniment, if desired

*H*ere is another cobbler done "Arnold's way." This dried peach version was inspired by some beautifully plump dried peaches found in one of our neighborhood's ethnic food shops.

1. In a 3- to 4-quart nonaluminum saucepan over medium heat, bring the dried peaches, water, and cider to a boil. Reduce the heat to low and gently simmer the peaches for 5 minutes, stirring occasionally, until the fruit is just tender but not soft and mushy. Remove the pan from the heat and let the peaches stand at room temperature until cool.

2. Preheat the oven to 425°F.

3. Drain the peaches in a colander set over a bowl and reserve the liquid. There will be 1 1/2 to 2 cups.

4. In a small saucepan, combine the reserved liquid and tapioca and let stand for 5 minutes. Bring the liquid to a full boil over medium heat, stirring often. Remove the pan from the heat and stir in both sugars, nutmeg, lemon juice, and butter.

5. In a 2-quart casserole, stir together the drained peaches and hot, thickened sauce. Let the mixture stand while you roll out the lattice strips.

6. Roll the pie dough into a 13-inch round and then cut eight 1 1/2-inch-wide strips. Before separating the strips, brush them with the egg glaze and sprinkle them with sugar. Arrange the strips in a lattice design over the warm peaches and trim them as directed in step 6 on page 189.

7. Bake the cobbler for 30 to 35 minutes, until the pastry is dark golden brown and the juices are bubbling.

8. Let the cobbler cool slightly on a wire rack before serving—with vanilla ice cream, if desired.

Brownie Pudding

Serves 5 or 6

THE PUDDING

1/4 cup plus 2 tablespoons
  unbleached all-purpose flour
1/3 cup granulated sugar
2 tablespoons unsweetened
  Dutch process cocoa powder
1 teaspoon baking powder
1/4 teaspoon salt
1/4 cup milk
1 tablespoon unsalted butter,
  melted
1/2 teaspoon pure vanilla
  extract
1/4 cup chopped walnuts

THE SAUCE

1/2 cup light brown sugar,
  firmly packed
2 tablespoons unsweetened
  Dutch process cocoa powder
3/4 cup boiling water

*T*here should be a brownie pudding in every recipe collection, and this one is Patricia's, copied down by her when she was ten or eleven years old from a pamphlet-type recipe booklet that her mother kept stored in one of the kitchen drawers. She's carried the recipe around for years, never losing it, and are we ever glad! This is a *singular* pudding. To begin with, the ingredients are available in any reasonably stocked kitchen; the mixing is simple, the baking quick. And the results are powerfully chocolaty: a warm chocolate pudding in its own rich sauce. This dessert must be accompanied by softened ice cream or whipped cream—just to relieve some of the chocolate intensity.

1. Preheat the oven to 350°F. Butter a 1-quart casserole or baking dish.

2. Make the pudding. In a medium bowl, stir together with a wire whisk the flour, granulated sugar, cocoa powder, baking powder, and salt. Sift these dry ingredients into a bowl and add the milk, melted butter, and vanilla. Stir to combine. Stir in the nuts.

3. Scrape the batter into the prepared baking dish and smooth the top with a spatula.

4. Make the sauce. In a small bowl, combine the light brown sugar and the cocoa powder. Sprinkle the mixture over the batter.

5. Pour the boiling water over the top of the batter and bake the pudding for 35 minutes.

6. Let the pudding cool slightly before serving.

Orange Caramel Cup Custards

Six 6-ounce custards

THE CARAMEL
1/2 cup water
1/3 cup sugar

THE ORANGE CUSTARD
1 cup whole milk
1 cup heavy cream
Three 2 × 1/2-inch strips of
  orange zest
3 large eggs
1/3 cup sugar
1 tablespoon Cointreau or other
  orange-flavored liqueur
1/2 teaspoon pure vanilla
  extract
Pinch of salt

*A*rnold and Michael like the flavor of orange and all of us like custard, so it came as no surprise at all that old-fashioned cup custards figured on each of our lists of most favorite desserts. These here, with their touch of liqueur, are sophisticated, rich, and creamy, but not eggy at all. You want to be careful handling the sugar syrup when coating the cups—it is hot and can burn. Aside from that, the preparation is easy and has to be done in advance to allow the custards to chill. The unmolding is straightforward, too. While custard is simple to make, it is a lovely dessert to serve after an elegant dinner. The hint of orange mingled with the flavor of caramel in this version produces a delicate and haunting result.

1. Make the caramel. Into a small saucepan, pour the water, add the sugar, and place over medium-high heat, swirling the pan gently to dissolve the sugar. Bring the mixture to a boil and boil rapidly until the water evaporates (the bubbles will be large and heavy) and the sugar begins to caramelize. Swirling the pan gently by the handle, continue cooking until the caramel is a pale golden color. Immediately remove the pan from the heat and pour about 2 teaspoons of the caramel into each of six 6-ounce custard cups. Quickly rotate each cup to coat the bottom. Let cool until the caramel is cool and hard.

2. Preheat the oven to 350°F.

3. Make the orange custard. In a small saucepan, combine the milk and heavy cream. Add the orange zest. Over medium heat, scald the mixture—small bubbles will appear around the edge of the pan and the temperature will be about 180°F. on a thermometer; do not let the mixture boil. Remove the pan from the heat and let steep for 15 minutes.

I'm doing just what I want to do. I don't have any urge to travel now, or go away. I look forward every day to coming to the Little Pie Company. It's what I want to do.

—A.W.

4. In a medium mixing bowl, beat the eggs with a wire whisk just until combined. (If beaten until they are foamy, the custards will have foam on top.) Stir in the sugar, liqueur, vanilla, and salt. Slowly stir in the milk and heavy cream mixture.

5. Strain the custard mixture through a fine sieve into another bowl, preferably one with a lip, or a large measuring cup.

6. Pour the custard mixture into the prepared cups, dividing it equally. Place the cups in a 13 × 9-inch baking pan and fill the pan with very hot—but not boiling—water to a depth of 1 inch.

7. Bake the cups for about 30 minutes, or until the custards test done when a knife inserted 3/4 inch from the edge comes out clean. (The center of the custard will quake if tapped, appearing undone, but will finish cooking outside of the oven.)

8. Immediately remove the custards from the water bath. Let cool, then cover and refrigerate for at least 4 hours or overnight.

9. To unmold, run a small knife around the edges of each cup, allowing air into the mold. Place a dessert plate over the custard cup and invert the custard and plate together. Lift off the cup. The caramel will have liquefied, making a sauce.

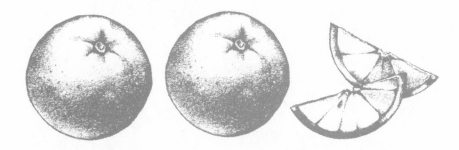

INDEX